CH GEDMAN • JASON VARITEK • JIMMIE FOXX • CAF
LT DROPO • BOBBY DOERR • JERRY REMY • PETE
CRONIN • NOMAR GARCIAPARRA • ROCEI
BOGGS • FRANK MALZONE • SHEA HILLENBRAND •
MANNY RAMIREZ • JIM RICE • MIKE GREENWELL •
LIS BURKS • JIMMY PIERSALL • DWIGHT EVANS • TON
R CLEMENS • CY YOUNG • PEDRO MARTINEZ • LUIS
Y GROVE • MEL PARNELL • BRUCE HURST • BILL LEE
KY LYLE • TOM GORDON • JOE McCARTHY • DICK
N FISK • SAMMY WHITE • BIRDIE TEBBETTS • RICH
STRZEMSKI • MO VAUGHN • CECIL COOPER • WALT
NELS • BILLY GOODMAN • CHUCK SCHILLING • JOE
• LUIS APARICIO • VERN "JUNIOR" STEPHENS • WAD
RNEY LANSFORD • GEORGE KELL • TED WILLIAMS •
MINIC DIMAGGIO • TRIS SPEAKER • FRED LYNN • ELI
NIGLIARO • REGGIE SMITH • JACKIE JENSEN • ROGEI
MENTE TIANT • TEX HUGHSON • BABE RUTH • LEFTY
CK RADATZ • BOB STANLEY • ELLIS KINDER • SPARK
MS • DON ZIMMER • ED BARROW • CARLTON FISK
ASON VARITEK • JIMMIE FOXX • CARL YASTRZEMSKI
BY DOERR • JERRY REMY • PETE RUNNELS • BILLY
R GARCIAPARRA • RICO PETROCELLI • LUIS APARIC

FEW AND CHOSEN

Defining Red Sox Greatness Across the Eras

Johnny Pesky

with Phil Pepe

TRIUMPH
BOOKS

CHICAGO

This book is dedicated to my dearest friends and teammates, Ted Williams, Bobby Doerr, and Dominic DiMaggio; to my lovely and wonderful wife, Ruthie, who has put up with me for more than 60 years; and to the hundreds of thousands of loyal and patient Red Sox fans who have waited so long to celebrate a World Series victory. Hopefully they will not have to wait much longer.

Library of Congress Cataloging-in-Publication Data

Pesky, Johnny, 1919–

    Few and chosen : defining Red Sox greatness across the eras / Johnny Pesky with Phil Pepe.

    p. cm.

    Includes index.

    ISBN 1-57243-608-5

    1. Boston Red Sox (Baseball team)—Biography. 2. Boston Red Sox (Baseball team)—History. 3. Baseball players—Rating of—United States. I. Pepe, Phil. II. Title.

GV875.B62P47 2004

796.357′64′0974461—dc22

2003063401

This book is available in quantity at special discounts for your group or organization. For further information, contact:

    Triumph Books

    601 South LaSalle Street

    Suite 500

    Chicago, Illinois 60605

    (312) 939-3330

    Fax (312) 663-3557

Printed in United States of America

ISBN 1-57243-608-5

Design by Nick Panos

All photos courtesy of AP/World Wide Photos except where indicated otherwise.

Contents

Foreword

I CAN HARDLY REMEMBER a time when I didn't know Johnny Pesky. When I came to the Red Sox in 1961, he was managing Seattle, their Triple A team in the Pacific Coast League, and I saw him in spring training. Two years later, he came to Boston and was my manager for two years, 1963–64. Later he would serve as a coach, a broadcaster, an assistant general manager, and again as manager, all with the Red Sox.

Pesky came to Boston 20 years before I arrived, and he's still there 20 years after I retired. Johnny's whole life has been baseball and the Red Sox. He does a tremendous job for the Sox in public relations as a kind of Red Sox ambassador—going all over, making appearances—and he still has time to go to spring training every year and to put on the uniform and hit fungoes before home games.

My one regret is that we never found out how good a manager he could have been. In his two seasons as Red Sox manager in the sixties, we weren't a very good team and we finished seventh and eighth in the American League. I did win my first batting championship under him in 1963, but I wish I could have done better for him. I wish he could have stayed around long enough to be the manager when the Red Sox got better and that he could have had the opportunity to show the world how good a manager he could have been with better players.

To me, Johnny Pesky is "Mr. Red Sox." He's been there longer than anybody and has been associated with more Red Sox players than anyone else, all the way back to his playing days alongside Ted Williams, Bobby Doerr, Jimmie Foxx, and Dom DiMaggio.

Because of his long association with the team, who better to choose an all-time Red Sox team than Pesky? And because he has been associated with every Red Sox player over the past 60 years, I am honored and flattered that Johnny has seen fit to find a place for me on that team at not one, but three different positions.

I think John has put together a pretty good team, and I'd like to make one suggestion. Let Johnny Pesky manage the lineup he has assembled, and then you'll see how good a manager he can be.

—CARL YASTRZEMSKI

Preface

As a boy growing up in Brooklyn, I was consumed by the game of baseball. I had my Dodgers, of course, and I followed them avidly in the
newspapers and through the warm, soft, syrupy Southern sound of Red Bar-
ber pouring like molasses through my radio. The idols of my youth had
names like PeeWee, Dixie, Cookie, and Dolph.

The Dodgers were number one in my young life. I saw my first game in
Ebbets Field at the age of six; watched my first no-hitter in 1946, pitched
against the Boston Braves in Ebbets Field by a Dodger with the unusual name
of Ed Head, who won only two other games that season; and cajoled my aunt
Anna to teach me long division before my peers learned it so I could figure
out batting averages.

In grammar school, I was introduced to gambling by an Arnold Rothstein
in training who financed an elaborate bookmaking operation. Put up 10 cents,
pick any three major league players, and if they combined for six hits on any
given day, you would get paid back at odds of 3-1. A return of 30 cents for a
dime! A windfall. And it seemed so easy for those of us who scoured the box
scores religiously.

Invariably, I would choose the top three hitters in the Boston Red Sox
lineup: Dom DiMaggio, Johnny Pesky, and Ted Williams. Occasionally, I
would throw in Stan Musial, but never when the Cardinals played the
Dodgers because it would be disloyal, and no doubt sinful, to root for Stan
the Man to get his customary three hits against my Dodgers. No good could
come from the filthy lucre I might have accrued in that fashion.

I felt no disloyalty in picking three members of the Red Sox, who didn't play in the same league as my Dodgers. I suppose if I had a second-favorite team, it was the Red Sox. After all, they wore a *B* on their cap, similar to that on the Dodgers' cap, and they were the fiercest rivals of the hated Yankees, who inflicted so much heartache on my young life. Mainly, I chose the three Red Sox hitters based on sound logic and my superior knowledge of the game that was unmatched by my peers and, no doubt, by any other 11-year-old on the planet.

Williams was Williams, the game's greatest hitter, a perennial batting champion who could be counted on to bat .350 or better in any season and get three hits in any game. I had only to hope that the day I selected him in my "hit pool" wouldn't be the day those cowardly American League pitchers would walk him three times.

I chose Dom DiMaggio, "the Little Professor," because as the leadoff hitter on the hit-happy Red Sox, he was almost certain to come to bat five times in any game, six on days the ball was rattling around Fenway Park.

Pesky was chosen because the man was simply a hit machine who was good for two or three hits on any given day. His name told you the kind of menace he was to pitchers. Pesky. It even became part of the baseball lexicon. A pesky hitter.

In 1942, his rookie season, Pesky batted .331 and was second in the league to—who else?—Ted Williams. Pesky led the league with 205 hits. There was no Rookie of the Year award in those days (it began five years later), but if there were, Johnny Pesky would have easily won it in the American League. Then along came World War II, and Pesky enlisted in the navy, was commissioned an ensign, and missed three of the best years of his baseball career.

He returned in 1946 and batted .335, third in the American League behind Mickey Vernon and Williams, and again led the league in hits with 208, including one stretch in which he had 11 straight hits. He also set an American League record by scoring six runs in a game. In 1947, Pesky again led the league in hits with 207, and his .324 batting average was third in the league to Williams and Barney McCoskey. Who's to say if it were not for the war, Pesky wouldn't have had more than 200 hits in each of his first six major league seasons?

A series of debilitating injuries prohibited Pesky from ever reaching the 200-hit mark again, but he batted over .300 in three of his next four seasons.

By 1952, he was no longer the player he once was, and the Red Sox traded him to Detroit, where he spent one season and parts of two others before finishing up with 49 games for the Washington Senators in 1954.

In a 10-year major league career, Pesky accumulated 1,455 hits, an average of 145.5 per season; had a lifetime batting average of .307; and struck out only 218 times in 4,745 at-bats.

Pesky started his baseball career as a Red Sox farmhand in 1940 and, except for a few years as a player in Detroit and Washington and as a coach with the Pirates and in the Yankees farm system, has been associated with Red Sox baseball for more than 60 years, longer than anyone else. That association is ongoing, as he remains to this day, past his 84th birthday, a Red Sox "coach" and special instructor. He can be seen at Fenway Park on game days hitting fungoes to infielders in pregame practice.

A member of the Red Sox Hall of Fame, Pesky has served the Sox as a minor league player and major league player, minor league coach and major league coach, minor league manager and major league manager, and radio-TV announcer. He played for Hall of Fame managers Joe Cronin, whom he replaced as Red Sox shortstop, and Joe McCarthy. He played alongside Hall of Famers Ted Williams, Jimmie Foxx, and Bobby Doerr, and he managed Hall of Famers Carl Yastrzemski and Carlton Fisk, as well as future Hall of Famers Roger Clemens and Wade Boggs.

All of which makes Johnny Pesky uniquely qualified to attempt the daunting task of selecting his all-time Red Sox team, five men at each position, plus the five best Red Sox managers.

Despite almost a century of disappointment (the Red Sox have not won the World Series since 1918 and have suffered through many near misses), some of the greatest players in baseball history have worn the Sox uniform—from Cy Young to Pedro Martinez, Babe Ruth to Luis Tiant, Lefty Grove to Mel Parnell, Tris Speaker to Dwight Evans, Rico Petrocelli to Nomar Garciaparra, Jim Rice to Manny Ramirez. And Johnny Pesky has seen and, in one capacity or another, been associated with most of them.

—PHIL PEPE
Englewood, New Jersey

Preface

ONE DAY EARLY IN 1960, I got a call from Harold Kaese of the *Boston Globe*, an old friend and a longtime Boston sports columnist. The result of that year's Hall of Fame voting by the Baseball Writers Association of America had just been announced, and Harold wanted to talk to me about it.

Harold took me a little by surprise. I hadn't been waiting by the telephone hoping I would get elected to the Hall of Fame. I didn't even know when the vote would be announced, and I had no expectation that I would be elected.

I knew I was eligible. I had fulfilled the requirement for election by playing in the major leagues for at least ten years, 1942–1954, and I had been retired for at least five years, having "hung them up" after playing for the Washington Senators in 1954. But I was a little startled to get Harold's call.

"Johnny," Kaese said, "I thought you'd get more votes than you did."

"How many votes did I get?" I wondered.

"One," he said.

His answer made me chuckle.

"Who's the writer that voted for me?" I said. "I want to send him a gift."

"How do you feel about getting only one vote?" Kaese said.

"Harold," I said, "I don't belong in the Hall of Fame. I wasn't that good. I had pretty good stats for 10 years, but not good enough. Look at the guys who are in there."

I never did find out who the writer was that voted for me, and I don't want to know. I'm grateful for his support, but should I be angry with those who didn't vote for me? There were 262 voters, which meant that 261 of them didn't consider me worthy of the Hall of Fame. In fact, no one was considered worthy that year.

In order for a player to be elected, he has to receive 75 percent of the votes cast. In 1960, that meant you needed 202 votes. So I missed getting elected by 201 votes. But I was in good company. Edd Roush, Sam Rice, Eppa Rixey, "Sunny" Jim Bottomley, and Ralph Kiner all were on the ballot that year, and none of them got the required 202 votes.

Through the years, many people have asked me about the Hall of Fame and have been kind enough to tell me they think I belong—more people now than when I was playing, so I guess I must be getting better. That flatters me. Sure, I would love to get into the Baseball Hall of Fame. Who wouldn't? But I can honestly say I never considered myself a Hall of Famer.

Marty Marion isn't in the Hall of Fame, and he was generally regarded as the best shortstop in the game in the forties and fifties. Luke Appling is in, but he played 20 years, had a lifetime batting average of .310, had 2,749 hits, and won two batting titles. He deserves to be in.

In my first few years with the Red Sox, people used to compare me to Phil Rizzuto and Pee Wee Reese. It wasn't quite on the same level as the arguments about whether Ted Williams was better than Joe DiMaggio, or who was the best center fielder, Mickey Mantle, Willie Mays, or Duke Snider, but there were debates, especially in Boston and New York, over which of us was the best shortstop. Rizzuto and Reese are both in the Hall of Fame, but I'm not. Phil and Pee Wee deserve to be there. I don't. I'm in the Boston Red Sox Hall of Fame, and that's good enough for me.

I didn't see Reese much, but I did see a lot of Rizzuto, and I think he was a better player than I was. I really do. I think I was as quick as Phil, and I didn't strike out a lot—I always put the ball in play. But I thought Phil was marvelous. I always loved him. I wish I could have been the ballplayer he was.

When Rizzuto and Reese were elected to the Hall of Fame, I was happy for them. I wish it could have happened to me, but it didn't bother me that they got in and I didn't. I was never jealous of anybody. I was just so happy to be playing big-league baseball. Here I was, a kid from Portland, Oregon, born of immigrant parents, playing in the major leagues. It was a dream come true.

I was born John Michael Paveskovich in Portland, Oregon, on September 27, 1919. I became Johnny Pesky when I was playing American Legion ball in and around Portland because the sportswriters said Paveskovich was a little hard to fit in a box score. It would look something like "P'skv'ch," so I had my name changed legally in 1947. My mother was not too happy about it, and I had to convince her it wasn't that I was ashamed of my name and my heritage. I'm proud of who I am and where my people came from, but Pesky was an easier name to pronounce and to remember. Eventually, she got used to it and enjoyed the attention when people called her Mrs. Pesky.

My mom and dad, Maria and Jacob Paveskovich, came to this country from the Austria-Hungary area, which became Yugoslavia after World War II. They were from a little town called Split. My father came to the United States first, with a group of his friends at the start of World War I, because they could get work. There was Pevaskovich, Babich, Stepavich, Bragavich, and Lolich, who happened to be Mickey Lolich's grandfather. They came here to make a living. They arrived in New York, stayed a while, and then moved west, working in logging camps and sawmills and finally settling in Oregon.

Once he was settled, my dad sent for my mother. Neither of them knew anything about baseball. The only thing my father did for exercise was play boccie. There were six kids in our family, three girls and three boys. I was fifth in line, the second of the three boys. Mom and Dad encouraged me to play sports. They were strict disciplinarians, and the only thing they asked of us was that we stay out of trouble and that they always knew where we were.

I went to a parochial school and was taught by nuns. They were wonderful women who would play catch with us during recess. That's how I started playing ball. Later I played in high school, Lincoln High, and then semipro, and eventually I was signed to play pro ball. In high school, I played baseball and hockey. I'm a frustrated hockey player. I wanted to play in the NHL, but I wasn't good enough.

While I was in high school, I played semipro baseball with two teams, Reliable Shoe and a hardware company, and I also played American Legion ball for a team sponsored by a restaurateur. In the summer of 1937, I played in a summer league in Bend, Oregon. In addition to our league games, we played against semipro traveling teams like the House of David and the Kansas City Black Cuban Giants. We'd play 40, 45, 50 games in the summer. In '38 and '39, we were in an American Legion tournament in Silverton, Oregon. We won the tournament in '39 and went to the national tournament in

Wichita, Kansas, with a team made up of high school and college kids and played against teams with pro ballplayers. We beat everybody and won the national American Legion championship.

The scouts started coming around. Cy Slapnicka, who signed Bob Feller and was the general manager of the Cleveland Indians, was in my house. Ernie Johnson, an old second baseman for the Yankees in the twenties who roomed with Babe Ruth—everybody roomed with Babe Ruth, I guess—was around a lot. He was a scout for the Red Sox. My mother really liked Johnson. He was a very well-dressed man, and he'd bring flowers for my mother and a bottle of bourbon for my dad. My dad wasn't a big drinker, but he liked a nip once in a while. When the scouts came, I'd have my older brother or my oldest sister there to interpret because my mother was embarrassed that she didn't speak the language.

In Silverton, I worked on the ground crew. My job was to drag the field and get it ready for the game. One day, I was marking the field and this big guy came up to me and said, "Is the Silverton team playing tonight?"

"Yeah," I said.

"Do you play?"

"Yeah."

"With whom?" he asked.

"Silverton," I said.

"What's your name?"

I told him, and he said, "I'm supposed to see you."

That night I got a couple of hits. The next night I got two more. I wound up leading the tournament in batting and winning the trophy for the best infielder. The big guy who had talked to me was a scout for the Cardinals, and after the tournament, he came up to me and said, "Well, kid, I liked what I saw. I'd like to sign you. Has anybody else been talking to you?"

I said, "The Red Sox, the Tigers, the Indians, the Cubs, the Yankees." I almost said "I'm a little bit in demand," but I didn't. I didn't want to sound too cocky. "I'm kind of leaning toward the Red Sox," I said.

He told me what the Cardinals would offer, and it was $1,000 more than the Red Sox were offering, so I got hold of my older brother, Tony, and told him about the Cardinals offer. Tony said, "You'd better take it up with Ma."

When I got back from Wichita, I told my mother about the Cardinals' offer, and she said, "No, no, no, you go to Boston with Mr. Johnson."

And that's how I signed with the Red Sox for a bonus of $500. I graduated from high school in 1939, and I started my professional career in Rocky Mount, North Carolina, in the Class B Piedmont League, in 1940. My salary was $150 a month. My first manager was Heinie Manush, a Hall of Famer, who led the American League in batting for the Tigers in 1926. He hit .378 that year and had a lifetime average of .330. Heinie Manush was very instrumental in my career. I learned a lot from him.

I went to my first spring training in Deland, Florida. There were 50 of us in camp, and for the first four or five days, all Heinie Manush did was walk around and observe. A few times I noticed him watching me take batting practice. He never said a word. At that time I wanted to hit like the big guys. I was 160 pounds, but I stood back in the box and held the bat down at the end. After about four or five days, Manush was watching me playing pepper. I was choked up on the bat, slapping the ball around, and he came to me and said, "Johnny, when you take batting practice, you can't hold that bat down at the end. You're a little guy. Those pitchers will knock the bat out of your hands. They're throwing 90 miles an hour."

"Ah, I'm strong," I said.

"Look," he said. "I just want to make a suggestion." He took me to the batting cage. Instead of standing back in the box, he suggested I move up in the box. Instead of holding the bat at the end, he told me to choke up. I found I had better control of the bat, and the next thing I knew I was hitting line drives all over the place. Line drive. Line drive. Line drive.

"This feels pretty good," I said.

"Just try hitting like that for a while," Manush said. It was the best advice I ever got. Manush really took an interest in me. He told me what I had to do in order to succeed and get to the big leagues. He was my biggest booster.

I wound up hitting .325 right out of high school and leading the league in hits with 184. Heinie told the Red Sox I was ready for the big leagues right then, but the next year, 1941, they sent me to Louisville in the American Association. I jumped from Class B to Triple A, and I got 195 hits and was voted Most Valuable Player in the American Association.

In 1942, the Red Sox brought me to Boston. More than 60 years later, I'm still in Boston, still associated with the Red Sox.

Baseball has been very good to me and, I think, I to it. It's the only thing I've ever done. I have been very lucky to have played professional baseball and to have played in Boston, which is such a great baseball town, and to have played for such a great organization as the Red Sox and for such a wonderful owner as Tom Yawkey, who did so much for my family and me. I have just one regret, and it's not that I'm not in the Hall of Fame. Given a choice between making the Hall of Fame and seeing the Red Sox win a World Series, I'd choose the latter. I want the Red Sox to win a World Series so badly. If that happens, I'd retire and just go to the games as a spectator.

I've never seen the Red Sox win a World Series. Few people have. I wasn't even alive the last time they won the World Series. It was 1918, the year before I was born.

Boston is a wonderful baseball city with wonderful baseball fans, and they've had so many disappointments.

There's a lot of luck involved in this game, and the Red Sox have never had any. We had an owner who was a song-and-dance man, and he had the greatest baseball player God ever created and sold him to the Yankees so he could finance his show, *No, No, Nanette*. In 1949, we needed to beat the Yankees one of the last two games to win the pennant, and Johnny Lindell hit a home run down the left-field line in the first game, and Jerry Coleman hit a ball off the end of his bat that fell in front of Al Zarilla in right field in the second, and we lost both games.

We lost in a playoff to Cleveland in 1948. There was the Bucky Dent home run in 1978, Bill Buckner's error in 1986, close calls in 1967 and 1975, and blowing a three-run lead with two innings to play in Game 7 of the 2003 American League Championship Series. Something always happens.

But there's a great baseball tradition in Boston, and I am proud to have been a small part of it. I've seen, played with, managed, and coached some of the game's greatest players—so many great players that trying to pick an all-time Red Sox team, the top five players at each position, is no easy job. In picking my team, there are outstanding players who unfortunately don't make the cut.

Some who played for the Red Sox I didn't see, but you didn't have to see them to know that Babe Ruth, Cy Young, Tris Speaker, and Lefty Grove deserve a place on the all-time Red Sox team.

In presenting my list, I have tried to be objective. But I have one disclaimer. Like anyone, I have my favorites—guys I played with, others I managed and coached—and I offer no apologies for favoring them.

—JOHNNY PESKY
SWAMPSCOTT, MASSACHUSETTS

Acknowledgments

THE AUTHORS ARE GRATEFUL for the cooperation and contributions of the following individuals: Gary Carter, Lou Piniella, Ralph Kiner, Rico Petrocelli, Bobby Doerr, Don Zimmer, Jim Kaat, Ken Singleton, Tom Seaver, Dom DiMaggio, Frank Malzone, and Reggie Jackson.

Our thanks also to Carl Yastrzemski and Ben Affleck, Chay Carter, Dick Bresciani and Keri Moore of the Red Sox, and to Mitch Rogatz, Tom Bast, and Blythe Hurley of Triumph Books' all-time team.

Introduction

THE HOUSE I GREW UP IN is less than two miles from Fenway Park. My father and I would walk there on summer afternoons when he couldn't find day work, and he'd buy us bleacher seats with a few crumpled dollars from his front pocket.

The bleacher seats at Fenway were heaven on earth to me. I would gaze out at the field (much more green than it looked on TV) and pepper my father with endless questions. One conversation we had stays with me to this day.

"Who's that guy hitting the fly balls?" I asked.

"That's Pesky."

"Who's Pesky? Why do they call him Pesky? Is he pesky?"

"No," answered Dad. "Well, maybe he's pesky, but that's also his last name. He used to be a player. Now he hits fly balls to the players and helps coach the team."

"When was he a player? When you were a kid?"

"Yeah. When I was a kid. The Red Sox made it to the World Series."

"No they didn't," I replied. "The Red Sox never make it to the World Series."

My father laughed. "They did and they will again. You'll see."

"So Pesky must be really old."

"He's not that old. He still hits fly balls, see?"

I mused on that for a minute. A glorious man from the golden age of Red Sox history, when they did things like make it to the World Series. This was better than the circus. And there he was, down on the great field of grass, cleanly swatting fly balls to these great ballplayers. What majesty this man must have, what power, what influence!

"Is Pesky the boss of Zimmer?" I asked.

"The Gerbil don't listen to nobody."

Dad was not a big Zimmer fan, though I always liked him (until he went turncoat and brought his band of pinstriped thugs to town and then tried to "wrassle" Pedro).

"I'll tell you what Pesky has that no one else has."

I went silent with anticipation. Well, I was silent for a half second, after which I felt Dad was really milking it, so I caved.

"What does he have?"

"He has that pole right there."

Dad pointed to the right-field foul pole, which was considerably closer to the action than we were.

"Why does he have that?"

"Because he is such a great man and so important to the team that they named the foul pole after him."

Dad neglected to mention that some people said it had something to do with the fact that Pesky hit more than his share of chip-shot home runs that hooked around that particular structure. So when people tried to convince me of that when I was 12, I knew they were lying.

"He has his own pole . . . named after him?"

"That's right."

I was thunderstruck. Jim Rice was the best home-run hitter on the team, and he didn't have a pole. Jerry Remy was my favorite player on the team because he was little and scrappy like me and gave me hope of one day playing for the Red Sox—and he didn't have a pole. The great Fred Lynn didn't even have a pole!

"What do they give the Rooster?"

"What do you mean?"

"Rick Burleson, do they give him a pole? Or an obstruction beam?" I knew that term because sometimes the only seats we could get were obstructed view. My father led me to believe that sitting there was a distinct honor bestowed on only a few fans—that sitting next to the "obstruction beams" was a privilege.

Dad thought for a minute. "No. They just give him money."

"So even the Rooster doesn't have a pole?"

Dad laughed again. I always liked it when he laughed, even though I never understood why he was doing it. Then again, it took me many years to understand what he and his friend Marty from the garage were really doing when they "rolled their own cigarettes," so I was used to letting things go that I didn't really understand.

"So nobody has anything except Pesky, who has a pole?"

"That's right," he replied.

"Even Pudge?"

"Even Pudge."

That sealed it for me, right there. I knew Ted Williams had a red chair (mostly because we always sat way behind it), but Pesky had a giant pole. And that's how I knew: Johnny Pesky was the greatest Red Sox player ever, bar none.

In 2002, I had the honor of walking through the Red Sox clubhouse during a rain delay. A team official was guiding me when I caught a glimpse of an older man wearing a Red Sox jacket. I stopped instinctively, and my guide turned to see what was wrong. He caught me staring slack jawed and evidently thought an introduction might be needed.

"Ben, this is . . . "

"You don't have to tell me who this is." I was eight years old again. "Mr. Pesky, it's an honor."

"Nice to meet you, son."

Time stood still. The earth stopped spinning. Of all the surreal, otherworldly things I've experienced in my life, this was by far the biggest. "Nice to meet you, son." That's what Johnny Pesky said to me. He was talking to me. He then ambled off into the locker room. That's when it hit me—my first real dream had just come true.

The "Pesky Pole" still stands in Fenway Park as a monument to the greatness of the Red Sox and their storied history. So does John Pesky.

—BEN AFFLECK

ONE

Catcher

THE MOMENT IS FROZEN IN TIME, vivid forever in the mind's eye of every long-suffering Red Sox fan. It was Game 6 of the 1975 World Series between the Red Sox and the Cincinnati Reds, "the Big Red Machine." Cincinnati was ahead in the Series, three games to two, and the score was tied, 6–6, as we came to bat in the bottom of the twelfth. We had been down to our final four outs, faced with elimination, when Bernie Carbo hit one of the biggest home runs in Red Sox history, a dramatic, pinch-hit, three-run shot in the bottom of the eighth to tie the score.

1. CARLTON FISK

2. SAMMY WHITE

3. BIRDIE TEBBETTS

4. RICH GEDMAN

5. JASON VARITEK

Neither team scored in the ninth, and the game went into extra innings, the tension, especially in Boston, building with each pitch, each base runner, and each out. The tenth inning was scoreless. So was the eleventh, thanks to a great game-saving catch by right fielder Dwight Evans who leaped high to take a home run away from Joe Morgan.

In the top of the twelfth, Rick Wise came in to pitch for us. He was the 34th player in the game and the 12th pitcher. Wise got the dangerous Johnny Bench to foul to **Carlton Fisk**, who made a nice catch leaning over the railing into the crowd. But Tony Perez and George Foster got back-to-back singles, and the Reds had runners on first and second. Wise got Dave Concepcion to fly to right and threw a third strike past Cesar Geronimo, and the Red Sox had dodged another bullet.

Fisk was the first batter in the bottom of the twelfth against right-hander Pat Darcy, the Reds' eighth pitcher of the game who had come in to pitch the tenth. On Darcy's second pitch, Fisk hit a towering drive down the left-field line. I was coaching at first base; Don Zimmer was coaching at third.

Though his famous World Series home run will always define his career, Carlton Fisk was so much more than a one-hit wonder. He's my runaway selection as the greatest catcher in Red Sox history.

When the ball was hit, I could see right away that it was deep enough and high enough to get over the left-field wall. There was no doubt it had the distance, it was just a matter of whether it would stay inside the foul pole. Because I was watching the ball, I didn't see Fisk's act in the batter's box, but I have seen the replay at least 100 times. Pudge was standing at home plate watching the ball. His body was leaning to the right, and he began to head for first base waving his arms toward right field as if to help keep the ball fair. The ball hit the foul pole, Fisk started skipping and hopping around the bases, and Fenway Park was going wild.

Pudge could do everything you want in a catcher. He could run (in 1972, he led the American League in triples with nine), he could throw, and he could hit with power. He called a good game behind the plate, was a great handler of pitchers, and, when he wasn't hurt, caught every day.

Fisk's home run, one of the most dramatic and maybe the most replayed home run in baseball history, won the game, 7–6, and forced a sudden-death seventh game, which we lost, 4–3, when Morgan hit a bloop single to center in the ninth to score Ken Griffey Sr. Another disappointment for the Red Sox.

For his home run alone, Fisk would merit a place on the all-time Red Sox team and in the Red Sox Hall of Fame. But Pudge was more than just a one-hit, one-game wonder. He had a Hall of Fame career and easily deserves to be selected as the greatest catcher in Red Sox history. No other catcher comes close.

Fisk's career spanned 24 seasons, 11 in Boston and 13 with the Chicago White Sox. He played in 2,499 games and caught more games, 2,226, than any other catcher in history. When he retired, Fisk had hit more home runs than any other catcher in history, 351 (although Mike Piazza will soon break that record).

Pudge could do everything you want in a catcher. He could run (in 1972, he led the American League in triples with nine), he could throw, and he could hit with power. He called a good game behind the plate, was a great handler of pitchers, and, when he wasn't hurt, caught every day. He didn't shirk his duties. Five times in his 11 years with the Red Sox, he caught more than 130 games. Twice, he caught more than 150. And he did it at the most demanding position on the field. That's why Pudge is in the Hall of Fame, where he belongs, and is first on my list of all-time Red Sox catchers.

After Carlton Fisk, it's pretty much a scramble among Red Sox catchers. The fact is, all other Red Sox catchers pale by comparison to Fisk. The Sox have

3

had a lot of good catchers, some who were excellent defensively, others who were pretty good hitters. But nobody comes close to Fisk as an all-around catcher, as they say in football, on both sides of the ball.

When I joined the Red Sox, catching was the weak spot in our lineup, and the team kept changing catchers, looking for someone who was not only a good receiver but who could contribute to the offense.

In 1941, the year before I got there, they had Frankie Pytlak, who had come over after nine seasons in Cleveland, and Johnny Peacock. In 1942, my first year, we had Bill Conroy, who hit .200, and Peacock. In 1943, it was Roy Partee. Then came the war years. When I returned in 1946, our catcher was Hal Wagner. In 1947, we had Birdie Tebbetts, who manned the position for four years. Then in 1950 came Matt Batts, who didn't. He hit .273 and had only four home runs and 34 runs batted in while splitting time with Tebbetts.

Sammy White spent seven years behind the dish for Boston; here he's catching against Mickey Mantle and the Yankees.

Despite arriving in Boston toward the end of his playing career, Birdie Tebbetts was still a .280–.290 hitter who solidified our catching for a few years. Here he's behind the legendary Joe DiMaggio.

After Batts, we got Les Moss, who came from the St. Louis Browns and batted .198. He shared the position with Buddy Rosar, who hit .229.

In 1952, the year I was traded, **Sammy White** was just breaking in. He batted .281 that year and went on to be the Red Sox catcher for the next seven years, usually batting in the .260–.280 range with from 10 to 15 home runs and from 40 to 70 runs batted in, which, at the time, made him the most productive catcher the Red Sox had ever had offensively. For that, I'll put him number two on my all-time list of Red Sox catchers.

I always had a soft spot for **Birdie Tebbetts**. He was a pretty good hitter and a good receiver, very smart. He wound up being a manager for Cincinnati, Milwaukee, and Cleveland, and for years he was a scout. He also was one of the great storytellers with that Irish blarney of his.

We got Birdie from Detroit in a trade early in the 1947 season, and he was a veteran catcher who fit in well with our team. He had spent eight as

Rich Gedman, Fisk's successor, was a fierce competitor and our mainstay behind the plate throughout the eighties.

the catcher for some pretty good Tigers teams. When we got him, he was 34 and didn't have a lot left, but he had all that experience and intelligence behind the plate, and he could still hit; he was a .280–.290 hitter without much power, and for a few years, he solidified our catching.

Rich Gedman might have been better served with another year or two in the minor leagues, but when Fisk left to sign with the White Sox, the Red

Sox had no other option at catcher, so they gave the job to Gedman. He always had a good left-handed bat—he hit 24 home runs in 1984 and had 18 home runs and 80 RBIs in 1985—and he made himself into a good receiver—good enough to spend 10 years as the Red Sox catcher and help them get to the World Series in 1986.

This kid we have now, **Jason Varitek**, has a chance to be an outstanding catcher. He's big and strong, 6'2", 210, and a switch-hitter. He reminds me a lot of Gedman in that he's a hard-nosed player, has a good home-run bat, and is a hard worker who has made himself into an excellent receiver. He plays the game the way it should be played, hard and without fear, which has cost him. He's been sidelined a lot with injuries. If he can stay healthy, he could be the best catcher we've had around here since Fisk

If he stays healthy—and stays in Boston—Jason Varitek could be the best catcher the Sox have had since Pudge.

or 19 years, from the mid-seventies, throughout the eighties, and into the nineties, Carlton Fisk and Gary Carter were contemporaries, the premier catchers in their respective leagues, Fisk in the American League, Carter in the National.

Their careers not only paralleled one another, their lifetime statistics are similar—Fisk played 2,499 games in 24 seasons and came to bat 8,756 times. Carter, in 19 seasons, played in 2,296 games and batted 7,971 times. Fisk was a career .269 hitter, Carter was .262; Fisk, with five more seasons, belted 376 home runs to Carter's 324 and drove in 1,330 runs to Carter's 1,225. Each made 11 All-Star teams. Fisk was elected to the Hall of Fame in 2000. Carter joined him three years later.

Although they never competed against each other, except in the All-Star Games of 1980, 1981, 1982, and 1985 and in spring-training games, they maintained a respectful rivalry as the standard bearers of their position in each league, and they had a mutual respect for the other's ability.

"On those rare occasions when we played against each other, I would watch Pudge's style," said Carter. "He was very methodical. Many times he was said to be like a human rain delay. Not taking anything away from his great talent in any way, but he was very descriptive behind the plate. He did everything in a slower way. That's just the way he caught, and it seemed most games were a little longer when he was behind the plate.

"Carlton had great talent. Obviously the longevity—he played 24 years, and he handled some great pitching staffs with Boston and then with the Chicago White Sox. It's hard to believe he played more years with the White Sox [13] than he did with the Red Sox [11] because, in your mind, you think of him in Boston, probably because he was a part of that dramatic 1975 World Series against Cincinnati, and he hit that home run off Pat Darcy to win Game 6.

"I admired Carlton, but I think there was a little bit of competition that went on through the years between us because I was representing the National League and he was representing the American League. But I had the ultimate respect for him. We both were with the Nike Company and we would go on these trips together. If you had won an MVP Award, or were an All-Star or won a Gold Glove or a Silver Bat, Nike, if you were part of their company, took you on these trips, so Carlton and his wife, Linda, and my wife, Sandy, and I became very close. We would interact and talk about different things and kid each other by comparing leagues.

"I remember one spring training playing against the White Sox in Sarasota. I was playing first base that day and a ball came up and hit me in the chest, and Carlton whistled to me and he held up a chest protector and said, 'Here, this is what you should be wearing.' So, there was a mutual respect, I think.

"Pudge had an unusual build for a catcher because he was so tall, about 6'4" (I'm 6'2"), and it's more difficult to get down in the crouch position and give a low target. But Pudge had such great flexibility, and he had great genes to be able to play 24 years as a catcher. Nevertheless, he always gave a good target and he called a good game. Don't forget, he had a knee injury early in his career [1974] that was so severe, they thought he might not play again. But he rehabbed it, came back, and had a Hall of Fame career."

Statistical Summaries

All statistics are for player's Red Sox career only.

HITTING

G = Games

H = Hits

HR = Home runs

RBI = Runs batted in

SB = Stolen bases

BA = Batting average

Catcher	Years	G	H	HR	RBI	SB	BA
Carlton Fisk *Set major league record with just four passed balls in 151 games in 1977*	1969, 1971–80	1,078	1,097	162	568	50	.284
Sammy White *Scored record three runs in one inning on June 18, 1953*	1951–59	981	881	63	404	14	.264
Birdie Tebbetts *Had exactly 1,000 hits in his 14-year career*	1947–50	419	404	19	189	17	.287

(continued)	Years	G	H	HR	RBI	SB	BA
Rich Gedman *Hit for the cycle on September 18, 1985*	1980–90	906	741	83	356	3	.259
Jason Varitek *Led all major league catchers with 1,049 total chances in 1999*	1997–2003	695	596	79	345	11	.265

FIELDING

PO = Put-outs

A = Assists

E = Errors

DP = Double plays

TC/G = Total chances divided by games played

FA = Fielding average

Catcher	PO	A	E	DP	TC/G	FA
Carlton Fisk	5,111	480	98	61	5.7	.983
Sammy White	4,458	482	76	79	5.2	.985
Birdie Tebbetts	1,568	201	35	33	4.4	.981
Rich Gedman	4,675	381	84	51	6.0	.984
Jason Varitek	4,398	274	38	32	7.1	.992

TWO

First Baseman

I WAS PRIVILEGED TO HAVE BEEN associated with some of the greatest players in baseball history, with Ted Williams, of course, being number one. And I am fortunate to have been a teammate, for one year, of another of the game's great sluggers, old double X, **Jimmie Foxx**, who was the first baseman when I joined the Red Sox in 1942.

At the time, only four men had ever hit 50 or more home runs in a season, when that was a rare and tremendous accomplishment. That was before the home-run explosion of recent years, with the smaller ballparks and stronger players and, maybe, a little help from the manufacturer causing baseballs to fly out of stadiums at will. Babe Ruth, of course, hit 50 or more home runs

1. JIMMIE FOXX

2. CARL YASTRZEMSKI

3. MO VAUGHN

4. CECIL COOPER

5. WALT DROPO

the most often, four times. Hack Wilson and Hank Greenberg each did it once, and Jimmie Foxx, Ruth's successor as the game's greatest slugger during the thirties, did it twice. He hit 58 with the Philadelphia Athletics in 1932 and 50 for the Red Sox in 1938, still the team record, and he hit at least 30 home runs for 12 consecutive years, a record that had lasted 62 years until it was equaled by Barry Bonds in 2003.

I feel fortunate to have had the privilege of playing alongside Jimmie Foxx, a wonderful person on and off the field and Babe Ruth's successor as the game's greatest slugger.

Foxx came to the Sox in 1936, when Connie Mack, the owner/manager of the Athletics, started selling off his big stars and Jimmie was still a productive hitter. In his first five seasons in Boston, Foxx hit 198 home runs.

The thing about Foxx is that he wasn't just a slugger. He batted over .300 13 times, twice led the American League in hitting, and had a lifetime batting average of .325 over a 20-year career. In 1938, when he hit 50 home runs, with 175 runs batted in, and a .349 batting average, he struck out only 76 times.

Ted Williams loved Jimmie and admired him as a hitter. We'd go into Detroit and Ted would stand in the dugout and point to the upper deck in left field and, in that booming voice of his so that all the players could hear him, including Foxx, he'd say, "See there, Foxx hit one up there." We'd go to Yankee Stadium and Ted would point to the bullpen in left-center field, about 450 feet away, and say, "Foxx hit one in that bullpen."

Foxx wasn't very big, about 6′ and 195 pounds, built kind of like Mickey Mantle, but he was very strong, and he could hit.

By the time I joined the Red Sox in 1942, Foxx was coming to the end of his career. His home runs had gone down from 36 in 1940 to 19 in 1941. The year I got to Boston, his eyesight was failing and he was striking out a lot. He was missing so many pitches, he just couldn't see. He even tried wearing glasses, but they didn't help. In June, he was sold to the Cubs, and he wound up hitting only eight home runs that year for both teams.

Foxx held on for two more years, finishing his career with the Phillies in 1945. That year, he played in only 89 games, mostly as a pinch-hitter, batted .268, hit seven home runs, drove in 38 runs, and retired after the season. He came back to Boston and had a radio show for a few years. I think Mr. Yawkey, the owner of the Red Sox, arranged for him to come back. Mr. Yawkey loved Foxx. Everybody did. What a guy. What a wonderful man.

Carl Yastrzemski is number two on my all-time list of Red Sox first basemen. Although he played that position just a short time, Yaz deserves to be mentioned as a first baseman as well as an outfielder. Twice, when the Red Sox needed a first baseman and had a surplus of outfielders, Yaz moved. He went there for one season in 1970 and then went back there for four seasons in 1973 when the trade for Danny Cater didn't work out. And he played a damn good first base.

By moving to first base from the outfield twice in his career, and playing there as well as or better than anybody else in the league, Carl Yastrzemski proved to me what a remarkable player he really was.

This tells me a few things about Yaz. He was a team player, a competitor, and a great athlete. He switched positions because the team needed him at first, and he worked hard and learned the position well enough to make the All-Star team as a first baseman.

I'll have more to say later about Yaz, who ranks second to Ted Williams as the Red Sox's greatest player.

Letting **Mo Vaughn** get away is one of the great tragedies of Boston base-ball—not as tragic as letting Babe Ruth get away, but right up there. When he left after the 1998 season, Mo was on his way to putting up Hall of Fame numbers. Losing him was bad not only for the Red Sox, it was bad for Mo, who hasn't been the same player since he left.

Mo Vaughn consistently put up Hall of Fame numbers while he was with Boston, but his career was never the same after the Sox let him get away.

Lou Piniella remembered the moment as if it were yesterday, although it was a lot of yesterdays ago. October 2, 1978. Fenway Park. Bottom of the ninth. Two outs. Runners on second and third. Piniella's Yankees leading their archrivals, the Boston Red Sox, 5–4. Carl Yastrzemski at bat against Goose Gossage with everything on the line—the game, and the American League East title.

"Yaz was the one guy you didn't want to see hitting in that situation," Piniella said. "Not only could he beat you with some power to right field, he could hit the ball off the left-field wall, he could hit the ball in the net. You didn't want him up there. I'm thinking I gotta be ready. He could hit a line drive my way.

"And then he hit that towering pop-up. It was a great confrontation, Yaz and Goose, both tough competitors. That's what baseball's all about.

"That pop-up. The ball seemed like it would never come down. I knew [Graig] Nettles was camped under it. I knew Nettles was going to catch it, but, boy, that thing just stayed up in the air forever. It seemed to me that time just stopped.

"Carl Yastrzemski was a great player. He not only had the ability to get it done on the field—his numbers speak for themselves—he also had the superstar flair about him. When I first came up to the big leagues in 1969, he was the player I liked the best. You could look at him, look at the way he carried himself, he had that superstar gait, that superstar flair.

"Carl had power, he could hit for average, he could steal a base, and he played the outfield well. I think of him as a left-handed Al Kaline. When I look at Carl's career, and I got a chance to play against Kaline, they were the two guys, one left-handed and one right-handed, that closely paralleled each other. Good athletes, could both hit, could both hit for power, and they looked like superstars on the field. They carried themselves like superstars. They played hard, they played to win, and they played on good teams. They were very similar.

"Neither of them was very big. That's the one thing about Yaz that surprised me. He was only about 5'11", but he was put together pretty good.

And he was a great athlete. He signed as a shortstop, and he became a great left fielder and a very good first baseman. He could play anywhere.

"What impressed me most about Carl—outside of the fact that he had a great career and he's a Hall of Famer—was that he made adjustments as he got older. He changed his batting style, and you'd see him two years later, and he changed it again. He kept changing to stay productive. Not too many players can do that. That's why he played until he was 44 years old. He had the ability to make adjustments and to compensate for the lack of bat speed at the end of his career, as he got older. He started holding the bat real high, and by the end of his career, his hands were right in close to the hitting area, lying on his front foot and shifting. It was good to see that transition because that's what you need to do to stay around a long time and have a great career like he had. Carl Yastrzemski was the heart and soul of that Red Sox team for a long time."

You would think that getting away from Fenway Park would have been good for Vaughn, a left-handed power hitter. But it wasn't. Mo thrived in Boston and was one of the most popular players ever to play for the Red Sox. The fans loved him, and small wonder they did. He hit at least 26 home runs for six straight years, including 39 in 1995, 44 in 1996, and 40 in 1998. He drove in 100 runs four times, including a league-leading 126 in 1995 and 143 in 1996. And he batted over .300 five straight years, including .337 in 1998, second in the American League.

Look at his final season in Boston, 1998. He had a .337 average, 40 home runs, and 115 runs batted in. With numbers like that, Vaughn thought he should get a long-term contract extension. Vaughn knew he was a good player, and he *was* a good player. He grew up in Connecticut and had made Boston his home. He wanted to stay, and the fans wanted him to stay, he was such a fan favorite. But the team had other ideas, and when the general manager refused to give Vaughn the kind of long-term contract he wanted, he walked away and signed with Anaheim. It was a mistake—a mistake by the Red Sox and a mistake by Mo.

In his first game with the Angels, he fell into the dugout chasing a foul pop and hurt his shoulder. He missed almost a month but still came back to hit 33 home runs and drive in 108 runs, and the next year he hit 36 homers and drove in 117. After that, he was traded to the Mets and had a terrible time in New York. His average slipped to .259, his home runs to 26, and his RBIs to 72. People said he was too heavy. But he always was heavy, 6′1″, and about 250 pounds, give or take 10 or 20 pounds. He's just a big man. He's heavy, but he's strong. He was heavy when he played for the Red Sox, but nobody complained about his weight back then because he was putting up big numbers in average, home runs, and RBIs. It's a funny thing in baseball; when you're hitting home runs, you're a big man, but when you stop hitting home runs, you're too heavy.

Not only was he a good player, Mo was a leader who was looked up to by the other players. He was great in the clubhouse. If you ever had a hassle in the clubhouse, he was right there, and he settled it. When it came to getting things squared away in the clubhouse, Mo Vaughn was the Ted Williams of his time.

Mo always could hit. He hit some balls as far as anybody. And he hit a lot of them. I don't care who the pitcher was—left-handed, right-handed, submariners, sidearmers—he hit them all.

When he came up, baseball people whom I respect in the game said he would never be a big-league ballplayer. I had a big-league manager tell me Vaughn would never be a big-league ballplayer. I told him he was wrong because I had seen what Mo could do. He became a good ballplayer when he got to the big leagues. He worked very, very hard in the minor leagues. He did a lot of work with his fielding, and he became a very good fielder with good hands because of all his hard work.

To me, Mo was an angel, small *a*, when he was with the Red Sox. We got along great because Mo knew I was in his corner. Not only was he a good player, Mo was a leader who was looked up to by the other players. He was great in the clubhouse. If you ever had a hassle in the clubhouse, he was right there, and he settled it. When it came to getting things squared away in the clubhouse, Mo Vaughn was the Ted Williams of his time. There is no greater compliment I can pay a player.

Cecil Cooper was another first baseman the Sox let get away. What a great kid he was. The reason the Sox let Coop leave was we had a good ballclub in those years, but we needed a right-handed hitter. So we traded Cooper to Milwaukee for George Scott, who had been with us before.

Cecil Cooper had some great years with the Sox early in his career, then flourished in Milwaukee after we had to trade him for right-handed batter George Scott. *Photo courtesy of Bettmann/Corbis.*

Scott had a couple of good years in his second tour of duty in Boston, but Cooper played 11 more years in Milwaukee and finished with a lifetime batting average of .298 for 17 seasons and helped the Brewers win a pennant.

Walt Dropo was one of those players who never got the credit he deserved. People thought of him as a big, strong, power-hitting first baseman who couldn't move and couldn't field. All he could do was hit home runs. They were wrong. Take it from me, Dropo worked hard to make himself into a better-than-average first baseman and hitter. I saw him tie a major league record by getting 12 straight hits, including 7-for-7 in a doubleheader against Washington. That was in 1952, the year he and I were both traded from the Red Sox to the Tigers.

Walt Dropo (right), with Vern Stephens (center) and Ted Williams, had an unforgettable
rookie season in 1950, batting .322 with 34 home runs and a league-leading 144 RBIs.
Photo courtesy of Bettmann/Corbis.

Walter was called "Moose," in part because he came from Moosup, Con-
necticut, and in part because he was a moose of a man, 6′5″ and 220 pounds.
He had an offer to sign with the Chicago Bears of the National Football
League, but he chose baseball instead.

When Jimmie Foxx left Boston, the Red Sox searched for his replacement for years and had a succession of first baseman, as if they had gone to First Basemen "R" Us to fill the position. In the World War II years, there were Tony Lupien, Lou Finney, and George Metkovich. After the War, they had Rudy York for a year, then Jake Jones and Billy Goodman. Then along came Dropo.

He came up in 1949, but he didn't hit and was sent back to the minor leagues. Walter worked hard in Louisville to improve, and when he returned to Boston in 1950, he was a different player. He batted .322, hit 34 home runs, led the American League with 144 RBIs, and was named Rookie of the Year. He also improved dramatically in the field. Unfortunately, he couldn't sustain that level of play and was traded two years later.

Statistical Summaries

All statistics are for player's Red Sox career only.

HITTING

G = Games

H = Hits

HR = Home runs

RBI = Runs batted in

SB = Stolen bases

BA = Batting average

First Baseman	Years	G	H	HR	RBI	SB	BA
Jimmie Foxx *Slugged grand slam homers in consecutive games on May 20 and 21, 1940*	1936–42	887	1,051	222	788	38	.320
Carl Yastrzemski *Collected more hits (376) and home runs (65) against Detroit than any opposing team*	1961–83	3,308	3,419	452	1,844	168	.285

(continued)	Years	G	H	HR	RBI	SB	BA
Mo Vaughn *Batted .412 with two homers and seven RBIs in 1998 Division Series against Cleveland*	1991–98	1,046	1,165	230	752	28	.304
Cecil Cooper *Was primary designated hitter on Red Sox 1975 A.L. Championship team (54 games)*	1971–76	406	377	40	181	12	.283
Walt Dropo *Led A.L. in total bases with 326 in 1950*	1949–52	283	307	51	229	0	.281

FIELDING

PO = Put-outs

A = Assists

E = Errors

DP = Double plays

TC/G = Total chances divided by games played

FA = Fielding average

First Baseman	PO	A	E	DP	TC/G	FA
Jimmie Foxx	7,126	614	69	707	9.7	.991
Carl Yastrzemski	6,459	512	41	610	8.7	.994
Mo Vaughn	7,842	544	99	785	9.1	.988
Cecil Cooper	1,762	122	22	168	8.7	.988
Walt Dropo	2,442	165	29	282	9.7	.989

THREE

Second Baseman

I FIRST LAID EYES ON **Bobby Doerr** in the summer of 1936, when he was 18 and playing second base for the San Diego Padres in the old Pacific Coast League and I was 16 and working in the clubhouse of the Portland Beavers. Little did I know at the time that six years later, I would be playing alongside Bobby in the infield of the Boston Red Sox—me at shortstop, him at second base—or that we would be teammates for almost 10 years and form a close friendship that is ongoing to this day, more than 60 years later.

I grew up only four blocks from Vaughn Street Park, where the Beavers played, and as kids, my friends and I would go to the ballpark there. The old groundskeeper, a man named Rocky Benevento, would let us play on the field when the Beavers were on the road as long as we helped him with his chores. When I was 12, Rocky Benevento put me to work. My job was to clean out the bullpens. By the time I was in high school, I was working in the visiting clubhouse, washing clothes and shining shoes and doing little chores for the ballplayers. I got paid in tips from the players, about $10 a week.

1. BOBBY DOERR

2. JERRY REMY

3. PETE RUNNELS

4. BILLY GOODMAN

5. CHUCK SCHILLING

When the game started, I would sit in the dugout during the game. That's how I got to see so many great players like Joe DiMaggio and Ted Williams. And that's also the first time I saw Bobby Doerr.

The general manager of the Red Sox, Eddie Collins, the Hall of Fame second baseman for the Chicago White Sox, came to Portland on a scouting mission. The Sox were looking for infielders, and they heard about George Myatt and Bobby Doerr. Collins signed Doerr, and it was on that same trip that Collins first saw Ted Williams and signed him. Myatt wound up signing with the Giants, and then he played for the Washington Senators, but he didn't have the career Doerr had.

Charlie Gehringer in Detroit and Joe Gordon, first with the Yankees and then with the Indians, were the big-name second basemen in the American League at the time, but Bobby was right there with them. He was a wonderful second baseman, smooth and steady.

Bobby played his entire career with the Red Sox, 14 years, from 1937 (five years before I got to Boston) until 1951 with one year in the service. He played in more than 1,800 games, every one of them at second base. He didn't play one game at another position in his entire major league career. Not one.

28

Charlie Gehringer in Detroit and Joe Gordon, first with the Yankees and then with the Indians, were the big-name second basemen in the American League at the time, but Bobby was right there with them. He was a wonderful second baseman, smooth and steady. He had great hands and was terrific at turning the double play. And what a hitter! He batted over .300 three times, drove in more than 100 runs six times, hit more than 20 home runs three times, and led the American League in slugging in 1944.

In 1946, when we had all come back after World War II, the Red Sox got off to a great start. Six weeks into the season we were 10 or 12 games out in front. Dominic DiMaggio was hitting .400, I was hitting .400, Williams was hitting about .600. But Bobby, for some reason, wasn't hitting as well as he should have been. Ted was his buddy; they were kids together. One day in Boston, we were waiting to get on the field. Ted was getting his picture taken for a magazine article, and Dom, Bobby, and I were in the dugout, waiting to take batting practice. After Ted got through with the photographer and the writer of this magazine article, he came down to the dugout. I can still see him and hear him.

"Bobby, get up here," he growled. "Goddammit, one time you've got the bat up here, another time you've got the bat down here. Open stance, closed stance, feet apart, feet together, what the hell's the matter with you?"

That's me on the right, congratulating my good friend Bobby Doerr on his 2,000th hit, on July 1, 1951, at Yankee Stadium.

*A*s a boy growing up in San Diego, Ralph Kiner remembers watching the Padres play in the Pacific Coast League and being impressed by a skinny, left-handed-hitting outfielder for the Padres named Williams and a tough, hard-nosed second baseman named Doerr.

Four years their junior, Kiner never knew or got to play with Ted Williams or Bobby Doerr. Their paths deviated when Kiner signed with the Pittsburgh Pirates and became the premier home-run hitter of his time in the National League, while Williams and Doerr spent their professional careers entirely in the American League. It wasn't until years later, after all three were elected to the Hall of Fame, that their friendship materialized and Kiner found a common ground with Williams and Doerr based on their great mutual passion, hitting.

"Bobby was a lot like Ted in that respect," Kiner remembers. "He loved to talk hitting, just like Ted, but he wasn't as loud or as headstrong as Ted was. They often disagreed on their approach to hitting, but they were very close. Doerr was probably closer to Williams than anyone who ever lived.

"They both loved to fish, so they had that in common, in addition to baseball. They grew up together as kids, played with the Padres together and then with the Red Sox."

Doerr got to Boston in 1937. Williams began his fabulous major league career two years later, and they were teammates for 10 seasons (Doerr spent one year in military service during World War II, and Williams spent three), until Doerr retired at the age of 33 after the 1951 season. Both played their entire major league careers with the Red Sox.

"I was in the National League [except for one season with Cleveland in 1955, after Doerr had retired]," said Kiner. "So I didn't get to see Doerr play, but I knew about him because he was a tough kid from Southern California. At the time, the two top second basemen in the American League were Doerr with the Red Sox and Joe Gordon with the Yankees and Cleveland. I always thought Gordon was the better of the two because he was more acrobatic in the field than Doerr was.

"They were comparable players, but Bobby is in the Hall of Fame and Gordon is not. Doerr was a good, solid hitter who did the job. He was usually in the .280–.310 range, he hit home runs, and he drove in a lot of runs. In the field, he wasn't as flashy as Gordon, but he was a hard-working, grind-it-out type of player.

"It wasn't until we'd get together for Hall of Fame week in Cooperstown that I got to know Bobby and found out how much he likes to talk about hitting, how much he knows about it, and what a good guy he is."

This went on for two or three minutes, and Bobby hadn't opened his mouth.

Finally, Ted said, "Get a good stance and give it a try."

Bobby looked him right in the eye and said, "But Ted, I'm not you."

And Ted looked at Bobby and roared, "If you want to be a .280 hitter, then be a goddamned .280 hitter." And with that, he stomped off.

Ted believed in that uppercut swing and was such a perfectionist, he would never settle for something like a .280 batting average, which would be good by today's standards. Bobby, on the other hand, had that downswing, and he and Ted argued all the time about their different approaches to hitting . . . or rather, Ted would do the arguing and Bobby mostly just listened. Ted would scream at Bobby all the time, "You're wrong, you're wrong." I can still hear him as if it was yesterday.

But Bobby didn't do much wrong. He wound up a career .288 hitter with more than 1,200 RBIs and more than 200 home runs. And it was Williams who led the campaign to get Bobby elected to the Hall of Fame in 1986.

Jerry Remy came within inches of being one of the biggest heroes in Boston Red Sox history. To refresh your memory, this came in the 1978 playoff game between the Sox and the Yankees, the game in which Bucky Dent hit that three-run home run and the Yanks beat us.

If you remember, the Red Sox had a 14H-game lead in July. Then several key players got hurt in the second half, including Remy, and the Yanks caught us. We ended the season tied for first place in the American League East, which forced a one-game playoff in Boston on October 2, the day after the regular season.

Jerry Remy's playing career was cut short because of knee problems, but he still ranks up there as the second all-time greatest Sox second baseman.

We were leading, 2–0, when Dent hit his three-run home run in the seventh inning. The Yanks scored another run in the seventh to make it 4–2, and Reggie Jackson hit a home run in the eighth to make it 5–2. But the Red Sox came back to score two in the eighth, and they batted in the bottom of the ninth, trailing, 5–4.

With one out, Rick Burleson was walked by Goose Gossage, and that's when Remy hit a screaming line drive to right field. Lou Piniella, the Yankees' right fielder, was blinded by the sun and never saw the ball, which landed in front of him. I can still see Piniella with his arms outstretched, groping for the ball. Somehow, the ball hit Piniella in the glove, and Burleson stopped at second.

With a little luck, the ball could easily have soared past Piniella and Burleson might have scored, or at least gone to third base with the tying run. At worst, we would have had runners on second and third with one out. Jim Rice followed with a drive that Piniella caught at the fence that would have scored Burleson from third to tie the game, and who knows what would have happened. We might have won the game and Remy would

Pete Runnels never batted below .300 in his five seasons with the Sox and won two batting titles during his 14-year career.

be hailed as a hero in Boston. What *did* happen was that Carl Yastrzemski popped up and the Yankees won the game. Another bad break for the Sox. Another disappointment.

Remy got still another bad break when knee problems hampered him and shortened his career, a career that had seemed to be on the way to establishing him as one of the best second basemen in the American League. In 1979

A lot like Runnels, Billy Goodman was another great-hitting, decent-fielding second baseman for the Sox.

Chuck Schilling was known for his sparkling defense, though this one off the bat of Minnesota's Jack Kralick got past him during his rookie year of 1961.

and 1980, he missed 179 games but batted .297 and .313 while playing less than half the time. He managed to play full seasons from 1981 to 1983, but the knee acted up again, and he played in only 30 games in 1984, and then retired.

Because of what he could have done, and what he did, Remy is my choice for number two on my all-time list of Red Sox second basemen.

Pete Runnels and **Billy Goodman**, numbers three and four among my all-time Red Sox second basemen, are so much alike it's as if they were clones. Both were outstanding left-handed hitters who knew how to take advantage of Fenway Park's Green Monster by taking the ball to left field with an inside-out swing.

Runnels was listed at 6', 170 pounds. Goodman was 5'11", 165. Runnels had a lifetime batting average of .291 for 14 years, Goodman an even .300 for 16 seasons. Neither of them was ever considered a good infielder, but they both were such good hitters, that managers moved them around the diamond just to try to keep their bats in the lineup. For example, in his career, Runnels played 644 games at first base, 642 at second, 463 at shortstop, 49 at third base, and 1 in the outfield. Goodman played 406 games at first base, 624 at second, 7 games at shortstop, 330 at third base, and 111 in the outfield.

Unfortunately, both came along before the designated hitter because they both would have been ideal DHs.

Goodman led the American League in batting with a .354 average in 1950. But Runnels won two batting titles (he's one of the few players to be traded the year after he won a batting championship, 1962, when he hit .326), and in five seasons with the Red Sox he never batted below .300. For that reason, I give Runnels a slight edge over Goodman.

Chuck Schilling and Carl Yastrzemski were rookies together in 1961, and both made an immediate impact on the Red Sox. Schilling was such a tremendous fielder, when he arrived he moved the defending American League batting champion, Pete Runnels, from second base to first. And Schilling was a dramatic upgrade at the position.

Unfortunately, Chuck's hitting didn't match his fielding, and he never came close to even equaling his rookie batting average of .259. When he began to put on weight, the Red Sox traded him to Minnesota after the 1965 season. Rather than play anywhere else but Boston, Schilling retired, after only five big-league seasons.

I would be remiss if I didn't acknowledge a few other second basemen who played for the Red Sox during my time there as a manager and coach—guys like Mike Andrews, Marty Barrett, Doug Griffin, and Dave Stapleton, all of whom came close to making my top five list and are worthy of a mention.

Statistical Summaries

All statistics are for player's Red Sox career only.

HITTING

G = Games

H = Hits

HR = Home runs

RBI = Runs batted in

SB = Stolen bases

BA = Batting average

Second Baseman	Years	G	H	HR	RBI	SB	BA
Bobby Doerr *Led A.L. second basemen in double plays a record-tying five times (1938, 1940, 1943, 1946, 1947)*	1937–44, 1946–51	1,865	2,042	223	1,247	54	.288
Jerry Remy *Collected 86 bunt hits during his Red Sox career*	1978–83	710	802	2	211	98	.286

(continued)	Years	G	H	HR	RBI	SB	BA
Pete Runnels *Led league in fielding at second base in 1960 and as a first basemen the following year*	1958–62	732	825	29	249	20	.320
Billy Goodman *Played in 149 games (599 at-bats) without hitting a home run in 1955*	1947–57	1,177	1,344	14	464	33	.306
Chuck Schilling *Hit pinch-hit home runs in consecutive at-bats on April 30 and May 1, 1965*	1961–65	541	470	23	146	11	.239

FIELDING

PO = Put-outs

A = Assists

E = Errors

DP = Double plays

TC/G = Total chances divided by games played

FA = Fielding average

Second Baseman	PO	A	E	DP	TC/G	FA
Bobby Doerr	4,928	5,710	214	1,507	5.9	.980
Jerry Remy	1,370	1,988	61	466	5.0	.982
Pete Runnels	820	963	28	274	5.3	.985
Billy Goodman	1,420	1,635	89	443	5.5	.972
Chuck Schilling	1,119	1,366	37	322	5.0	.985

FOUR

Shortstop

After one year with Rocky Mount in the Piedmont League and one year with Louisville in the American Association, I found myself, at the age of 21, in spring training with the Red Sox, competing for a job with the big club and thinking, "This is too quick." In those years, you had to go from league to league to league before you got a shot at the big leagues.

So I figured I didn't have a chance to make the Red Sox. I thought I would be sent back to Louisville, but all the writers were saying it was between me and Eddie Pellagrini, who was a couple of years older than I was. One of us was going to make the club. Eddie was in the Pacific Coast League with San Diego in 1941, and he hit 19 home runs but batted only

1. Joe Cronin
2. Nomar Garciaparra
3. Rico Petrocelli
4. Luis Aparicio
5. Vern "Junior" Stephens

about .270. I was with Louisville, and I hit .325, led the league in hits and runs, and was the Most Valuable Player of the American Association.

The manager of the Red Sox was giving us both a fair shot. He'd play me one day, Eddie the next, then me again, then Eddie. And we'd play all nine innings because we were rookies and the manager wanted to get a good look

Joe Cronin, my first manager in the major leagues and my predecessor at shortstop, became one of the most accomplished men in the history of the game.

at us. About the middle of spring training, Eddie came up lame, and we had to play the Cardinals and the Yankees on successive days in St. Petersburg. With Pellagrini out, I had to play both games.

I had a good day against the Cardinals, and the next day we played the Yankees. I got a base hit off Lefty Gomez, who was coming to the end of his career. I hit a line drive over the head of Yankees second baseman Joe Gordon for a single, and when I got to first base, Lefty looked over at me and said, "You little piss pot, I must be through if I can't get you out." I took that as a compliment.

The Yankees and Red Sox always played tough games and always tried to beat one another, even in spring training. Late in the game, about the seventh inning, I was playing short and Joe DiMaggio hit a rocket in the hole. I took two steps to my right, backhanded the ball, and threw him out at first base. I felt pretty good about it, and I thought for sure the manager was going to say something to me. But he didn't say a word.

After a few days, Pellagrini was ready to play, and so we went back to alternating at shortstop, him one day, me the next. Then it was time to cut the roster to 25 men and Pelly was sent to Louisville. But nobody had said anything to me. I figured I was next.

We broke camp, and I was still with the ballclub as we went north, stopping on the way to play four games against Cincinnati, and I was playing every day, all nine innings. We played in Atlanta, and then Memphis, and the last of the four games was in Lexington, Kentucky. Johnny Vander Meer, the only man in baseball history to pitch consecutive no-hitters, was pitching for the Reds. He was a hard-throwing left-hander, and he was mean. About the sixth inning, Vander Meer threw me a curveball that hung up there, and I hit it to right-center field for a triple. The manager came up to me after the inning and said, "Kid, you just made the ballclub."

The manager of the Red Sox that season, 1942, was **Joe Cronin**, who also happened to be the shortstop in Boston for the previous seven years. But he was 35 at the time, and he was ready to step down and concentrate on managing, even though he had batted .311, hit 19 home runs, and driven in 95 runs the year before. So when I took over at shortstop for the Red Sox in 1942, I was playing for a man who was not only my manager, but also my predecessor, a future Hall of Famer, and one of the most accomplished men in the history of baseball.

41

Garciaparra is part of the new breed of shortstops. In my day, shortstop wasn't an offensive position. The shortstop usually was a little guy who was there primarily for his fielding. Anything he hit would be considered a bonus. He didn't hit for much power; he just kind of slapped the ball around. Today, shortstop has become an offensive position with players like Alex Rodriguez, Miguel Tejada, Derek Jeter, and Nomar—big guys who in my day probably would have played another position.

By the time he came to the Red Sox as player/manager in 1935, Cronin was already a star for the Washington Senators and the premier shortstop in the game. In 1930, the year before the baseball writers began voting for the Most Valuable Player, Cronin was named Player of the Year in the American League by *The Sporting News* for his .346 batting average, 13 home runs, and 126 runs batted in. In 1933, at the age of 27, he was named manager of the Senators, and he led them to the American League pennant. Two years later, he was sold to the Red Sox by Washington owner Clark Griffith, who was Joe's uncle-in-law.

Cronin continued as a player/manager with the Sox, batted over .300 in four of his seven full seasons in Boston, drove in more than 100 runs three times, and hit more than 15 home runs five times. And he managed the Red Sox to a pennant in 1946. He left the field after the 1947 season and became general manager of the Red Sox, a position he held until 1959, when he was elected president of the American League. He was the first former player to become a major league president, a position he held for 14 years.

There will come a time, not too far in the future, when **Nomar Garciaparra** will supplant Joe Cronin as the number one shortstop in Red Sox history. Not yet. Maybe not until Garciaparra is elected to the Hall of Fame.

Already, after only eight seasons, Nomar has put up the kinds of numbers that few shortstops in the game's history have put up. His lifetime batting average is almost 30 points higher than Cronin's, he's won two batting titles (Cronin didn't win any), and he's already hit more home runs than Cronin hit in 20 seasons. But he's still only about halfway to Cronin's RBI total.

Garciaparra is part of the new breed of shortstops. In my day, shortstop wasn't an offensive position. The shortstop usually was a little guy who was there primarily for his fielding. Anything he hit would be considered a bonus. He didn't hit for much power; he just kind of slapped the ball around. Today, shortstop has become an offensive position with players like Alex Rodriguez, Miguel Tejada, Derek Jeter, and Nomar—big guys who in my day probably would have played another position.

Nomar Garciaparra, with his striking offensive numbers, is among the new breed of shortstops and will one day supplant Cronin at the head of this list.

Rico Petrocelli was as talented a player as we've ever had in Boston, but a series of injuries limited his potential and forced him out of the game at age 33.

44

I first saw **Rico Petrocelli** when I was the manager of the Red Sox's Triple A team in Seattle and I was sent to Florida to work with young players at a 15-day minicamp. Ted Williams was there to work with the hitters, Charlie Wagner worked with the pitchers, and Eddie Popowski and I worked with the infielders. Petrocelli was this skinny kid from Brooklyn, a third baseman at the time, and he stood out. There were two fields back-to-back, and one day he opened our eyes by hitting a ball over both fields.

Popowski and I spent a lot of time hitting ground balls to Petrocelli. One day, Pop said, "You know, Johnny, we ought to try this kid at shortstop." He had great hands, a strong arm, and good range, so we moved him over, and he was the Red Sox shortstop for seven years, until we got Luis Aparicio and moved Petrocelli to third. Rico did a great job at third base, too—led the league in fielding the first year he played third.

Rico Petrocelli never thought of himself as a trailblazer, a shortstop who could hit the ball out of the park (40 home runs in 1969, still the Red Sox record for shortstops) and drive in runs (103 in 1970). Until Petrocelli hit 40 home runs, Ernie Banks was the only shortstop to hit 40 home runs in a season. Two years after he did it, Banks was moved to first base.

Petrocelli was the Red Sox shortstop from 1965 through 1970, and he might have continued at that position if the Sox didn't have a chance to get the great Luis Aparicio.

"They were looking for a third baseman at the time," Petrocelli recalled. "They couldn't get one, but they had a chance to get Aparicio. They called me and asked me if I would move over to third base. They said they had a chance to get Luis Aparicio and they figured I'd have to move to third base eventually, why not now.

"I said, 'Yeah, great.' I was excited about playing alongside Aparicio. He was older, at the end of his career, but he was still an amazing shortstop. I played next to him for three years, and he was fantastic."

First Banks, and then Petrocelli, changed the concept of what a shortstop could, and should, be.

"It used to be that they thought a shortstop was a guy who sprayed the ball around and was fast, had good range, and was an excellent fielder," Petrocelli said. "After I hit the 40 home runs, I think that opened some eyes. I read articles where managers were saying, 'Wait a minute, that's not a bad idea. If you've got a big guy who's athletic and can pop the ball out of the park and knock in some runs, there's no reason he can't play shortstop.' Now you have big guys like [Derek] Jeter, A-Rod [Alex Rodriguez], [Miguel] Tejada, and Nomar, who can hit the ball out of the park."

Some 30 years after he played shortstop for the Red Sox, Rico Petrocelli's voice was filled with pride when he talked about Nomar Garciaparra, who holds down the position today.

"I was with him in the minor leagues, when I was a roving instructor for the Red Sox," said Petrocelli. "In addition to his God-given athletic ability, the thing that impressed me about Nomar was his great work ethic. He wanted to be better, and he worked hard to improve. In Trenton, he would go under the stands and hit in the batting cage for a couple of hours, *after* the game. He didn't show major league power back then [only eight home runs in 125 games at Trenton], but he went on a workout regimen and got bigger and stronger.

"Even in the minor leagues, Nomar had that ritual he goes through before every pitch. When he went up and down the dugout steps, he would go one step at a time, first with his left foot, then his right foot on each step. I asked him, 'What are you doing?' and he said, 'I've got to do that.' Occasionally, I would watch him when he went to the bat rack. If he was in the middle of the dugout, and he'd have to walk to the end of the dugout, he'd make the sign of the cross 175 times before he got to the bat rack."

Petrocelli knows there's a good chance that someday soon Garciaparra will break his Red Sox record for home runs as a shortstop (Nomar hit 35 in 1998).

"I wouldn't feel bad if he does it," Petrocelli said. "I honestly wouldn't. If he does it, he would deserve it. I have great respect and admiration for him. He's a great kid, very respectful and caring. Whenever I go to Fenway Park, Nomar comes over to me and gives me a big hug.

"I get the feeling that Nomar wants to leave Boston. Since the Red Sox have had so many disappointments, the press can be hard on a player. I just hope Garciaparra stays here and doesn't go someplace else when he becomes a free agent. If he does, the people of Boston are going to realize how great a player Nomar was and how hard it's going to be to replace him."

Petrocelli was as good a ballplayer as we've ever had in Boston. And he was a tough kid. I loved him.

In 1969, he hit 40 home runs, which was an American League record for a shortstop at the time. Of all the shortstops in baseball history, only Ernie Banks had hit more. That same year, Petrocelli tied an American League record for the fewest errors by a shortstop, 14.

He was still young, at the top of his game, when injuries took their toll on him. He had elbow problems, then a leg injury, and he was hit in the head with a pitch, which caused him to have inner-ear problems that forced him to retire after the 1976 season. He was only 33 at the time.

I know **Luis Aparicio** played only two seasons for the Red Sox, but I have to put him fourth on my list. I thought Aparicio was the best shortstop I ever saw. He was around for 18 years and played more games at shortstop (2,581) than anybody else in major league history. I saw him make plays nobody else made. And he wasn't a bad hitter, either, with more than 2,600 major league hits. He led the American League in stolen bases in each of his first nine seasons, but it was primarily his defense that got him elected to the Hall of Fame and, to me, sets him apart from all other shortstops I've seen.

Because his defense rates him among the greatest shortstops of all time, people forget that Luis Aparicio was a more-than-decent hitter as well. Unfortunately, he spent only two seasons with the Red Sox—but he still makes my list.

Vern Stephens, shown here tagging out Stan Musial in the 1949 All-Star Game, put up the kind of offensive numbers more suited to today's bigger breed of shortstops.

After the 1947 season, the Red Sox made a trade with the St. Louis Browns, who needed money. We sent them six players and $310,000 for Jack Kramer and **Vern "Junior" Stephens**. Stephens was a star with a bad team, the Browns. He led the league in home runs one year and in RBIs another year. We got him for his bat, but shortstop was his normal position, and I wondered where he was going to play with us.

About a week or 10 days into spring training, our clubhouse man Johnny Orlando came to me and said, "Mr. McCarthy wants you."

Joe McCarthy had taken over as manager from Joe Cronin that spring, so I went to see him, and he said, "Johnny, I want you to go over to third base." That's all he said: "You work out at third base."

So I went over to third and started taking ground balls there. McCarthy later told me the reason he put me over there was that I had a better glove hand than Stephens had. They could have stuck me in right field and I would have gone there. I just wanted to play.

Now when I look back, I see it was a compliment to me that McCarthy thought I could make the adjustment from shortstop to third base. I think he didn't want to disturb Stevie. We got him for his bat, and I think McCarthy wanted him to stay where he was comfortable so as not to lose his offense. And he did a great job hitting for us, batting behind Ted Williams in the lineup and giving Ted the kind of protection that forced pitchers not to walk him too often. They had to respect Stephens hitting behind Ted, just as they respected Jimmie Foxx, Walt Dropo, and Rudy York.

Stephens was a strong kid. In his first three years with us, he hit 29, 39, and 30 home runs and drove in 137, 159, and 144 runs. He led the league in RBIs in 1949 and 1950.

Stevie and I got to be good friends. For a while, we even roomed together on the road.

In 1951, after McCarthy left and was replaced by Steve O'Neill, I moved back to shortstop and Stevie went to third, and it worked out better for us.

I've run out of room on my top five list of all-time Red Sox shortstops, but I couldn't forgive myself if I didn't at least make mention of Rick Burleson, "Rooster," who was our shortstop for seven seasons and was the heart and soul of the Red Sox infield in the seventies.

For the first three years of his Red Sox career, shortstop Johnny Pesky played alongside a future Hall of Fame second baseman, Bobby Doerr, who saw up close and appreciated what a good double-play partner he had.

Doerr had been in place as the Red Sox second baseman for five seasons when Pesky joined the team in 1942 and made an immediate impact by lashing out 205 hits. Pesky went off to military service for three years, but he picked up right where he left off when he returned to bang out 208 hits in 1946 and 207 in 1947, and he combined with Doerr to give the Red Sox skill and production out of their double-play combination.

"Johnny was a very good shortstop," said Doerr. "Outstanding. He had a good arm, good hands, and good range. He wasn't a flashy guy, just a good, steady shortstop who didn't make a lot of errors. He didn't make the spectacular play, but he made all the routine plays, and that's what you want in a shortstop."

In 1948, Doerr had a new double-play partner. Vern Stephens, who had been acquired in a trade with the St. Louis Browns, took over at short; Pesky moved to third.

"That was [Joe] McCarthy's idea," said Doerr. "He never said why he made the switch. Pesky was a good third baseman, but he was a better shortstop than Stephens, and we would have been better off the other way, with Pesky at short and Stephens at third."

The experiment lasted until 1951, Doerr's final year in Boston, when Steve O'Neill took over for McCarthy and restored the natural order of things—Pesky to short, Stephens to third. But the three years playing third base eroded Pesky's shortstop skills, and he was traded to Detroit the following season.

"I think it hurt Johnny moving to third," said Doerr. "He didn't get a chance to show how good a shortstop he was. If he had played eight or ten years there, he would have gotten more credit as a shortstop. He might have made the Hall of Fame. He was as good as [Phil] Rizzuto and [Pee Wee] Reese, a better hitter than either of them, and they're in the Hall of Fame.

"Another thing that hurt Johnny as far as making the Hall of Fame was that he didn't play in as many World Series as Reese and Rizzuto. Pesky played in only one [1946], and he was made the goat of that World Series [for holding the ball while Enos Slaughter scored the winning run]. But he shouldn't have been the goat. Reese and Rizzuto would have done the same thing."

In 1978, when we led the American League East by 14H games in July and the Yankees caught us, Burleson got hurt late in the season. He missed 18 games completely and played hurt a lot of games. I truly believe if Burleson had not been hurt, there would have been no tie with the Yankees, no play-off game, and no Bucky Dent home run.

Statistical Summaries

All statistics are for player's Red Sox career only.

HITTING

G = Games

H = Hits

HR = Home runs

RBI = Runs batted in

SB = Stolen bases

BA = Batting average

Shortstop	Years	G	H	HR	RBI	SB	BA
Joe Cronin *Holds A.L. season record of five home runs as a pinch-hitter (1943)*	1935–45	1,134	1,168	119	737	31	.300
Nomar Garciaparra *Thirty-game hitting streak in 1997 longest ever by an A.L. rookie*	1996–2003	928	1,231	173	669	82	.323
Rico Petrocelli *Hit two home runs in Game 6 of 1967 World Series*	1963, 1965–76	1,553	1,352	210	773	10	.251

(continued)	Years	G	H	HR	RBI	SB	BA
Luis Aparicio *Hit leadoff home run on May 1, 1971; next batter, Reggie Smith, also homered, the first Red Sox teammates to perform that feat*	1971–73	367	361	7	133	22	.253
Vern Stephens *Led A.L. shortstops in assists three times and double plays once*	1948–52	660	721	122	562	7	.283

FIELDING

PO = Put-outs

A = Assists

E = Errors

DP = Double plays

TC/G = Total chances divided by games played

FA – Fielding average

Shortstop	PO	A	E	DP	TC/G	FA
Joe Cronin	1,767	2,691	221	565	5.2	.953
Nomar Garciaparra	1,413	2,640	130	517	4.6	.969
Rico Petrocelli	1,283	2,283	113	433	4.8	.969
Luis Aparicio	567	1,046	53	178	4.6	.969
Vern Stephens	873	1,635	75	396	5.1	.971

FIVE

Third Baseman

WHEN YOU MAKE YOUR LIST of baseball's great hitters, be sure to put the name **Wade Boggs** on that list. Very high on that list.

I'm not saying Boggs is as great a hitter as Ted Williams, who's in a class by himself, or that he can be compared with Babe Ruth, Henry Aaron, Mickey Mantle, or Barry Bonds. They were home-run hitters, power guys. Boggs was not a home-run hitter. He could hit home runs. He hit 24 one year. Boggs was what we call a "pure hitter," in a class with people like Stan Musial, Rod Carew, George Brett, and Tony Gwynn.

Boggs' approach to hitting was to use the whole field and hit the ball hard somewhere. He had that inside-out swing, and most of the balls he hit hard, he hit to left field. He hit everybody: right-handers, left-handers, sidearmers, knuckleballers. And you couldn't strike him out. The most he ever struck out in one season was 68, but usually he was in the 30s and 40s in strikeouts, and that's fantastic these days.

1. WADE BOGGS

2. FRANK MALZONE

3. SHEA HILLENBRAND

4. CARNEY LANSFORD

5. GEORGE KELL

Boggsy had more than 3,000 hits, a lifetime batting average of .328, and he won five batting titles, including four in a row. He was as good a pure hitter as I've ever seen. When his time comes, in a couple of years, he's a sure bet to get elected to the Hall of Fame, and I'd like to be there in Cooperstown to help him celebrate the occasion.

As much as I like him as a hitter, the thing about Boggs that I'm proudest of, and what I admire most about him, is how much he improved his defense.

As much as I like him as a hitter, the thing about Boggs that I'm proudest of, and what I admire most about him, is how much he improved his defense. When he first came up, he was just an average third baseman with good hands but without a strong throwing arm. He wanted to become better, and he worked hard to improve.

When he first came up, he was just an average third baseman with good hands but without a strong throwing arm. He wanted to become better, and he worked hard to improve. He worked harder than anybody I've ever seen, and I know about how hard he worked because when I was coaching, it was my job to hit him ground balls before the game. I must have hit him thousands of ground balls. Every day at 3:00. And it was exactly at 3:00 because Boggs was fanatical, maybe even superstitious, about doing everything the same time every day. He ate the same pregame meal every day at the same time, came onto the field every day at the same time.

Cookie Rojas was in town one day scouting for Toronto, and he came over to say hello. Cookie is a baseball lifer like me. He was an outstanding second baseman for the Phillies and later a coach and then a scout. We got to talking about Boggs, and Cookie said he was scouting when I was coaching and he remembered seeing me hitting ground balls to Boggs every day.

It wasn't until late in his career, when he was with the Yankees, that all that hard work paid off for Boggs and he won his first Gold Glove. He won it two years in a row. When he won his first one, in 1994, he told the writers the reason he got the Gold Glove was because "in Boston, Pesky hit me ground balls every day."

Seeing that quote in the newspapers meant a great deal to me.

I have a soft spot for **Frank Malzone**. I thought he was a terrific player, and he's one of my favorite people. I have a great affection for Malzy. In the two years I managed the Red Sox, he was as good a ballplayer as I had under my command. We weren't very good in those years, but Malzone never complained. You never heard a peep out of him, and he played every day. He came to the Red Sox in 1955 and has been with them ever since, except for one year with the Angels. He still works for the Sox as a scout.

Wade Boggs was as good a pure hitter as they come, but what I loved most about him was how hard he worked to improve his defense—he even eventually became a Gold Glove winner.

Frank was born in the Bronx, and one of the few satisfactions Red Sox fans have over the Yankees is that we got some pretty good players out of New York, like Carl Yastrzemski, Rico Petrocelli, Chuck Schilling, Ben Ogilvie, Jerry Casale, and Frank Malzone, most of them signed by an old left-handed pitcher named Bots Nekola.

Malzone was a tough New York kid and a durable player. In a four-year span, from 1957 to 1960, he missed only four games. In an eight-year period, he missed only 43 games. Frank played on some mediocre Red Sox teams in

Frank Malzone was a Gold Glove winner for three straight years and made eight All-Star teams despite playing on some pretty forgettable Red Sox squads.

the fifties and sixties, but he won the Gold Glove for third basemen three straight years and made eight All-Star teams.

After Boggs and Malzone, who manned third base for the Red Sox for more than 20 years between them, the pickings are slim for Red Sox third basemen. Remember that some of the better third basemen in Red Sox history have been players who moved over from shortstop, such as Rico Petrocelli and Vern Stephens [editor's note: and Johnny Pesky], and they were discussed at their primary positions.

The rest of my top five are three players who were in Boston just a short time but still made their mark. **Shea Hillenbrand**, number three on my list, is another one of my favorites. Maybe I'm getting a little personal here, because Hillenbrand is like a son to me. What a good kid he is. He reminded me of Malzone as a third baseman, and he reminded me of Boggs because he worked so hard to improve his fielding. Just as I did with Boggs, I hit thousands of ground balls to Hillenbrand, and his defense improved dramatically.

He was here only two-and-a-half seasons, but he made a great impression on me. He's a good fielder and a good hitter, and I thought he was going to be a solid third baseman for the Red Sox for a long time.

When they traded him to Arizona, I was heartbroken. I was close to tears when I heard the news. I don't think you trade an everyday player who could hit you 25 home runs a year for a lot of years for a pitcher, unless that pitcher is a potential 20-game winner.

Like Boggs, Shea Hillenbrand was a player I worked with closely to improve his defense. He was only with us for a few years, but he was one of my favorite players and made a lasting impression on me.

When he managed the Red Sox in the late seventies, Don Zimmer kept hearing about "this kid in Pawtucket, a third baseman who could really hit."

The kid's name was Wade Boggs.

"I didn't know who Wade Boggs was at the time," Zimmer remembered. "I had never seen him. They told me he could hit but wasn't a very good fielder."

By the time Boggs got to Boston, Zimmer had moved on to Texas as manager of the Rangers, so he never had the chance to manage Boggs, but he saw enough of him as a manager in the other dugout. He saw too much of Wade Boggs.

"He was a lot better third baseman than I had been led to believe," Zimmer said. "He was sound. He was sure-handed, and he had a strong, accurate arm. He wasn't Brooks Robinson, but who the hell is? He didn't have great range, but he caught everything hit at him. He didn't make a lot of errors. And he got a zillion hits."

More than a decade after he left Boston, Zimmer hooked up with Boggs when Zim became Joe Torre's bench coach with the Yankees and Boggs came to New York as a free agent and won two Gold Gloves as a Yankee.

"He did it with hard work," Zimmer said. "Wade Boggs was a hard worker at everything he did. He made himself into a .300 hitter, which must be a wonderful feeling. I never had it [Zimmer was a lifetime .235 batter for 12 major league seasons]."

The one criticism of Boggs has been that he didn't hit many home runs, only 118 in an 18-year career, although he once hit 24 in a season.

"I always wondered why he didn't hit more home runs," Zimmer said. "He could have if he wanted to. I watched him hit balls out of Yankee Stadium in batting practice. If you put him in a home-run-hitting contest, he could win it if he wanted to.

"When I first saw Henry Aaron, he was such a good hitter, I thought he could lead the league in batting seven out of ten years, but then he started hitting home runs and his batting average declined."

Aaron led the National League in batting in 1956, his third season, with a .328 average but only 26 home runs. The following year, he led the league with 44 homers and was fourth in batting. He would win just one more batting title, but he became baseball's all-time home-run king.

"Sometimes, you can't have both," said Zimmer. "If Wade Boggs had tried to hit more home runs, his average might have dwindled. He had that good inside-out stroke, and he had the left-field wall in Fenway Park, so he learned to hit the ball to left field off that wall.

"The manager will decide when a hitter moves a runner along. Man on second, nobody out in a close game, the manager will tell the third-base coach to give the hitter the sign to hit the ball to right field and move the runner. With Boggs, I'd say to Joe [Torre], 'Let's not ask him to move the runner. Let's take his line-drive single to left field, then we'll have runners on first and third with nobody out.' And that's what we did."

I was very upset when I first heard that we had traded Hillenbrand to the Diamondbacks. That was my immediate reaction, and I admit it was personal, kind of like they had traded my own son.

Once it sank in and I thought about it objectively, I could understand the trade. We needed a relief pitcher very badly and we got one from Arizona. At the same time, it opened up third base for Bill Mueller, a switch-hitter we had signed as a free agent—and darned if this kid Mueller didn't win the American League batting title and help the ballclub a great deal.

So, despite my personal feelings, I guess trading Hillenbrand was not a bad thing for the Red Sox. Mueller looks like the real deal, but after one year, it's too soon for me to rate him among the Red Sox's five best third basemen.

I see the Diamondbacks are playing Hillenbrand at first base. I think that's a mistake. I still think he can be a very good major league third baseman. But whatever position he ends up playing, mark my words, Shea Hillenbrand is going to be a very good player in this league for a long time.

The Red Sox got **Carney Lansford** in a trade with the Angels in 1981, and right away that trade paid off. Lansford won the batting title in his first season in Boston, the first right-handed hitter to lead the American League in batting in 11 years. The next season, he again batted over .300.

Carney Lansford was also with the Sox for only a brief period of time, but he had a great glove and he won a batting title in his first season in Boston.

The year after that, Lansford was traded to Oakland for Tony Armas, a trade the Red Sox made for only one reason—to make room at third base for Wade Boggs.

Lansford went on to have an excellent career with the Athletics, but how can you fault the Red Sox for trading away a player who would be replaced by Wade Boggs?

Speaking of being replaced, **George Kell** and I exchanged places in 1952. George came to Boston from Detroit, and I went to Detroit from Boston in a nine-player deal that also included Walt Dropo going to the Tigers and Dizzy Trout and Hoot Evers coming to the Red Sox.

When the Red Sox got Kell, he had already carved out a Hall of Fame career with the Tigers with six consecutive seasons over .300, including a batting title in 1949, when he beat Ted Williams out on the final day of the season by .0001. Williams had gone hitless on that day. If he had gotten just one hit, Ted would have been the only player in baseball history to win the Triple Crown three times (he and Rogers Hornsby are the only players who won two Triple Crowns).

When the Red Sox got him, Kell was still a productive hitter. He batted over .300 both seasons he was in Boston, and then he was traded to the White Sox for Grady Hatton.

Practically a Hall of Famer already when he came to the Sox from Detroit, George Kell (right) once beat Ted Williams (left) for the batting title by .0001, denying "Teddy Ballgame" what would have been his record third Triple Crown. Here Kell turns over his uniform jersey to manager Lou Boudreau in 1954 after hearing he'd been traded to the White Sox.

Statistical Summaries

All statistics are for player's Red Sox career only.

HITTING

G = Games

H = Hits

HR = Home runs

RBI = Runs batted in

SB = Stolen bases

BA = Batting average

Third Baseman	Years	G	H	HR	RBI	SB	BA
Wade Boggs *187 of his team record 240 hits in 1985 were singles*	1982–92	1,625	2,098	85	687	16	.338
Frank Malzone *First Red Sox player to win a Gold Glove (1957)*	1955–65	1,359	1,454	131	716	14	.276
Shea Hillenbrand *Ranked in A.L. top 10 in at-bats, hits, and doubles in 2002*	2001–03	344	365	33	170	7	.284

(continued)	Years	G	H	HR	RBI	SB	BA
Carney Lansford *In 1981 became first right-handed Red Sox player to win batting crown in 43 years (since Foxx '38)*	1981–82	230	279	15	115	24	.317
George Kell *Led A.L. third basemen in fielding seven times*	1952–54	235	253	18	123	5	.305

FIELDING

PO = Put-outs

A = Assists

E = Errors

DP = Double plays

TC/G = Total chances divided by games played

FA = Fielding average

Third Baseman	PO	A	E	DP	TC/G	FA
Wade Boggs	1,165	2,956	177	299	2.8	.960
Frank Malzone	1,270	2,824	188	286	3.2	.956
Shea Hillenbrand	215	525	44	43	2.5	.944
Carney Lansford	153	379	23	36	2.8	.959
George Kell	333	634	40	63	3.0	.960

SIX

Left Fielder

ALL RIGHT, I NEVER SAW BABE RUTH or Rogers Hornsby or Ty Cobb or "Shoeless" Joe Jackson, but I have seen just about all the other great hitters in baseball history, and I'm telling you nobody was better than **Ted Williams.** Nobody!

You know about the .406 batting average, the last player to hit .400, the .344 lifetime batting average (sixth highest in history), and the two Triple Crowns (Williams and Hornsby are the only players ever to win two Triple Crowns). You know about the six batting titles (the last when he was 40 years old), the 2,654 hits, and the 521 home runs. You probably also know about the five years he lost fighting for his country in two wars—five years in the prime of his career, three years in World War II when he was 24 and had just won two straight batting titles, and two years in Korea, when he was 31.

> 1. TED WILLIAMS
>
> 2. CARL YASTRZEMSKI
>
> 3. MANNY RAMIREZ
>
> 4. JIM RICE
>
> 5. MIKE GREENWELL

Had he not missed those five years, he probably would have won at least two more batting titles, maybe more; he would have had more than 3,000 hits; and, based on his average of 30 home runs a year, he would have had 671 home runs, second in history at the time and close enough to challenge Babe Ruth's record of 714.

I can't say enough about Ted Williams, as a hitter, but also as a man, a teammate, a friend, and a national hero. True, he was bombastic, opinionated, cantankerous, stubborn, loud, and volatile. But that was all part of the Williams charm. He also was loyal, compassionate, generous, and considerate—someone you could go to and depend on if you needed help.

True, he was bombastic, opinionated, cantankerous, stubborn, loud, and volatile. But that was all part of the Williams charm. He also was loyal, compassionate, generous, and considerate—someone you could go to and depend on if you needed help.

I first encountered Williams when I was working in the clubhouse for the Portland Beavers in the Pacific Coast League and he was a skinny, 19-year-old kid playing for San Diego. I actually heard about Williams before I ever saw him. You'd hear the players talking about some young guy who was coming into the league, and I kept hearing about this skinny kid with San Diego named Williams who could really hit, and when he came to Portland, I saw for myself. I couldn't believe the power he generated from that skinny frame. Even then, the other players were in awe of him, and even then, he would hold court with the other players and talk hitting, and his was always the loudest voice.

I didn't have any conversations with Williams back then. I was just a kid, working in the clubhouse, and I would shine his shoes, wash his socks, and straighten his uniform. Little did I know that I would be playing alongside him five years later.

Dominic DiMaggio was in the league at that time, playing for the San Francisco Seals, and he told the story about the first time Lefty O'Doul saw Williams. Lefty, who was managing the Seals, had won two National League batting championships, one with Philadelphia and one with Brooklyn, and Dominic said the first time O'Doul saw Williams hit in batting practice, he went over to him and said, "Kid, don't let anybody ever change your swing." And he walked away.

Eddie Collins, the general manager of the Red Sox, came to look at Bobby Doerr and George Myatt in 1937, and he saw Williams. The story goes that when it came time to make a purchase from the San Diego ballclub, the Red Sox were going to buy two guys, and everybody thought it would be the double-play combination of Doerr, the second baseman, and Myatt, the shortstop. Collins went to the owner of the San Diego club and said, "I want

The two greatest and most beloved players in Boston history—Ted Williams (left) and Carl Yastrzemski—held down left field for the Red Sox for more than 30 combined years.

the second baseman and the guy in left field," and the Padres' owner said, "You don't want the guy in left field; he's nuts." And Collins said, "I don't care, I want the kid in left field."

That's how the Red Sox got Ted. They sent him to Minneapolis as a 19-year-old in 1938, and he hit 43 home runs and batted .366. Then they brought him to Boston in 1939, the year I signed with the Red Sox. I was in Louisville when he hit .406. The next year, 1942, I was his teammate. That spring, I was having dinner with Bobby Doerr, and Williams, who was late getting to spring training that year, showed up and joined us.

"You're the kid from Portland, right?" said Williams.

"That's right," I said.

"They tell me you're a pretty good hitter."

"That's right," I said, because I had 195 hits in Louisville and I was a little cocky at the time.

"Well if you can hit .280, you can help us," Williams said.

"Hell, I can do that just running out infield hits," I said.

Well, I hit .331 that first year, 1942, and I guess I proved myself to the great man because we became good friends—Williams, Doerr, DiMaggio, and me. They called us "the Big Four." We all came from the West Coast. I was the last of them, and I'm the youngest.

Bobby and Dominic were the quiet guys. I used to chirp back at Williams once in a while. I'd jabber at King Farouk. He was the King. He took over. He loved Bobby, and he loved Dominic, and I was a throw-in. He liked me, too. He used to say I was awfully dumb, and I accepted it.

He was the smartest man I've ever known, and the orneriest and most complex. There were times I loved him and times I wanted to kick him in the shins.

One day, we were playing the Yankees, and pitching for them was Spud Chandler, who was as mean as any pitcher I ever faced. He was mean on and off the mound. I came across him when he was playing in the Pacific Coast League and I was working in the Portland clubhouse. He was mean and nasty then, too.

Chandler had a hard sinker that I just couldn't hit. I'd try to pull it and wind up hitting a ground ball to second baseman Joe Gordon.

Before the game, a reporter named Jack Mullaney stopped by my locker and told me I was 0-for-14 lifetime against Chandler. Williams heard this, and he came over and said, "For Christ sakes, don't try to pull this guy."

*I*n 1957, Mickey Mantle battled Ted Williams late into the season for the American League batting championship, which Williams won by hitting a redoubtable .388 at the age of 39 to Mantle's .365. It was the highest average of Mantle's career and, although he was a fierce competitor, he was not distraught at finishing second. The previous year, he had beaten out Williams, .353 to .345, when he won his only batting crown (and the Triple Crown), and Williams was the hitter Mantle most admired.

Williams had started slowly in 1956, while Mantle was scalding hot in the first half of the year, but by August, it had become a race. Mantle went into a slide and Williams had cut into Mantle's huge early lead and was breathing down his neck when the two teams met on August 14 for a three-game series in Yankee Stadium.

"I had never won a batting title and I wanted it badly," Mantle said years later. "But I knew Williams, no matter how old he was, was going to make it tough for me to win it. I would rather be chased by any player but him. But then, if I was going to lose the batting championship, I wanted to lose it to the greatest hitter who ever lived."

As the dog days of August dragged on, Mantle continued in a slump, his batting average falling through the .370s and .360s into the .350s, and Williams continued in hot pursuit. Mantle pulled out of his slump in the final days of August, and when the month ended, his average was back up to .367, and he had a healthy lead on Williams.

But September started badly for Mantle, and midway through the month, Williams inched in front in the batting race. The lead changed hands twice in a three-game series between the Yankees and Red Sox, but Mantle heated up in the final week and won the title. Asked how it felt to lose the batting title to Mantle, Williams responded, "If I could run like that SOB, I'd hit .400 every year."

Mantle talked frequently of his admiration for the Red Sox slugger.

"I always liked going to Boston," Mantle once said, "because it was a chance to see Ted Williams hit. He's the greatest hitter I ever saw, and I always enjoyed watching him swing the bat, even against us. Any chance to see Williams hit was a thrill for me. Also, the rivalry between the Yankees and Red Sox, and their fans, was so strong that the games were fun."

Mantle also liked playing in All-Star Games, he said, "because I got to be a teammate of my idol, Ted Williams, even if it was just for a day. It was a thrill for me just to be on the same team with him, just as it was a thrill to be on the same team with Joe DiMaggio. They are the two greatest players I ever saw: Williams the greatest hitter, Joe the greatest all-around player.

"When we got together at All-Star Games, I used to love to talk to Williams about hitting—or rather listen to Williams talk about hitting because, with Ted, you didn't get to do much talking. He did all the talking in that loud, booming voice of his. I listened to him and I watched him in the batting cage, and it was like a clinic.

"Williams loved to talk about hitting. He would do it for hours, or as long as anybody was there to listen. It was his favorite subject, next to fishing, and he made a science out of hitting—all that technical stuff that I didn't understand. Hell, I just used to go up there swinging. About the only thing I understood about hitting was that you looked for the ball and hit it as hard as you could.

"Williams liked to talk to other hitters and ask them their theories, things that he might be able to apply and use himself. He was always asking questions, looking for new theories on hitting, telling his own theories, anything to learn more and improve. One time he asked me which was my power hand, which hand I used to guide the bat. I had no idea what he was talking about, but for several days after our conversation, I started thinking about all the things he told me. I was thinking so much, I didn't get a hit for a week."

We went to the seventh or eighth inning tied, 1–1, and I came to bat with two runners on base—Bill Conroy on third and Dominic on second—and two outs. I had already been 0-for-2 in the game, so I was 0-for-16 against Chandler.

Bill Dickey went to the mound to talk to Chandler, and Williams was in the on-deck circle, and he said, "You know he's going to throw you that hard sinker. Now don't try to pull it. You know goddamned well they're not going to walk *you* to get to *me*."

He was right. With Williams batting behind me, I always got good pitches to hit. I should have hit .300.

The count went to 2–2, and here came that hard sinker. Instead of trying to pull it, I slapped it the other way. Red Rolfe was playing in on the grass, and Phil Rizzuto was playing in the hole, and I just hit it between them. I couldn't have placed it better if they let me go out and roll the ball. Conroy scored, and DiMaggio scored. And we went ahead, 3–1.

I was standing on first base and Chandler was mad as hell, looking over at me and cursing me out. "You little son of a bitch, the next time I'm going to stick one in your ear."

I just looked back at him and said, "You were a lousy tipper when you were in the Coast League."

Ted was standing at home plate listening to all this, a big grin on his face. Then he hit Chandler's first pitch nine miles into the seats. When he came into the dugout, Ted was still smiling. "Boy," he said, "that felt good. Where's that little needle-nosed shortstop? I told you that you can't try to pull that guy."

I just looked at Ted and said, "He was so damn mad at me, he forgot you were the next hitter."

I remember the last time I saw the big guy. I got a call in October of 2001 from Dominic DiMaggio, who said he was going to drive down to Florida to see Ted, and he asked if I wanted to go with him. I said I did. Bobby Doerr couldn't make it from Oregon because his wife was sick and he needed to stay home to care for her.

There were three of us—Dominic, me, and Dick Flavin, a television personality in Boston—and we set out for Florida from Massachusetts, with a stop in Philadelphia.

When we finally got to Ted's home and we saw him, I almost had a heart attack. He was in a wheelchair, and he looked so frail and weak, it broke my heart. Here was a guy who had been the picture of health and strength as a young man; you could never imagine him looking so frail. He must have been less than 150 pounds.

Once I got over the initial shock of seeing him so sickly, we had a wonderful visit. Dominic, who has a fine singing voice, sang a song to him that made Ted smile. We told stories and had him laughing and, as he always did, Ted picked on me. He said I was dumb and called me "needle nose."

I knew when we left him that we probably would never see him again. It was a sad ride home, but a happy one, too, because we knew our visit meant so much to him. As sad as it was to see him like that, I'm glad we made the trip.

The following July, I was at home, and my wife, Ruthie, and I were playing gin rummy. It was 11:00 in the morning; the television was on, and they interrupted the program to report that Ted Williams had passed away at his home in Florida. It was July 5, 2002.

The next thing I knew, my telephone was ringing and people were asking for my reaction to Ted's death. Then my house was swarming with television cameras and reporters. I was doing a television interview, and I couldn't get through it. I just broke down talking about him. I had to stop and collect myself before I could continue.

We were Ted's family—Dominic, Bobby, and I. We had a wonderful association for more than 60 years, until Ted passed away.

74

If Ted Williams had a deficiency as a ballplayer, it was his defense. Not that Ted couldn't play defense. He just was so absorbed with hitting that he didn't work as hard on defense as he might have. He did learn to play the Green Monster very well, but not like **Carl Yastrzemski**, who played it like he built it. Nobody played the left-field wall in Fenway like Yastrzemski. He also had a better arm than Williams.

Between the two of them, Williams and Yastrzemski held down left field for the Red Sox for more than 30 years.

It's unfortunate for Yaz that, for the purposes of picking an all-time Red Sox team, he has to be compared with Williams. They're my two favorites and the two greatest and most beloved players in Boston history.

Williams is Williams. There's only one Teddy Ballgame, and Yastrzemski has to play second fiddle to him. But I have a way to remedy that and give Yaz his due, which I will discuss in a future chapter.

Manny Ramirez is as good a right-handed hitter as I've ever seen. He's got such a great swing, and he's a very intelligent hitter.

Very few right-handed hitters lead the league in hitting, but Manny did it in his second year with the Red Sox. And he's an RBI machine.

Manny Ramirez (right) is as good a right-handed hitter as I've ever seen, and he's taught himself how to play the Green Monster well enough to rank third on my all-time list. Here he's greeted by Nomar Garciaparra after a two-run homer in May 2003.

In Ramirez's first two years in Boston, the Red Sox used him half the time as their DH. But Manny has too much pride to be half a ballplayer. In Cleveland, he was the everyday right fielder, but the Red Sox put him in left field, and he had to learn how to play the Green Monster. He worked hard to improve his defense, and he became a good left fielder. I've seen him make some great catches.

Manny is still a young guy, just a few years over 30. He's still got a lot of good years ahead of him. I just hope the Red Sox can afford to keep him when his contract runs out. If they do, there's no telling what he can accomplish.

To me, Manny Ramirez is a latter-day **Jim Rice**. They're a lot alike—big, strong RBI machines and great right-handed hitters with great swings. The difference between them, I guess, is that the game has changed. It's more of a power game today, and guys are hitting more home runs because the ballparks are smaller and the ball is livelier. In his day, Rice was the premier right-handed power hitter in the league.

Jim Rice succeeded Yaz to continue the string of Hall of Fame–caliber left fielders in Boston. He hasn't gotten his call yet, but I feel that he belongs in Cooperstown.

Jimmy was a devastating hitter who should be in the Hall of Fame. He had a lifetime average of .298 for 16 seasons, batted over .300 seven times, was the MVP of the American League in 1978, and led the league in RBIs twice and in home runs three times. He drove in more than 100 runs eight times and hit 39 or more home runs four times in the days when nobody was hitting 50 home runs.

I had one writer tell me he wouldn't vote for Rice for the Hall of Fame because he wasn't a good guy. Maybe he was tough on the writers, but to me, Jimmy was a pussycat and a great teammate, very popular with other players.

When Don Zimmer was the manager and I was one of his coaches, my job was to work with Rice every day. I was his hitting instructor, but he didn't need a hitting instructor. What could I tell him?

But I'd take him under the center-field bleachers, and he'd take batting practice. Then I'd take him to left field and I'd hit him ground balls and balls off the wall so he could get used to the way the ball caromed off the Green Monster. I didn't care what the weather was, cold, warm, he was out there every day and he learned to play left field.

Rice always had a strong arm, but when he first came here he would throw the ball sidearm and you never knew where the ball was going. In spring training the year after his rookie season, when the workout was over, I'd get a pocket full of balls and go behind third base, and Rice would go to left field and I'd just hit him fly balls.

One day, Dwight Evans had been getting in some extra running, and he stopped to take a breather and was talking to Rice. Evans finished his running and came up to where I was hitting the balls, and I said, "Go down there and see if you can get Jimmy to throw the ball overhand." Evans went back and talked to Rice about it. Jimmy started throwing the ball over the top and, sure enough, his throws were coming in strong and true, and that must have convinced Rice, because from then on, he threw the ball overhand. And the next two years he led the league in assists.

For nearly 60 years, four men—Williams, Yaz, Rice, and **Mike Greenwell**—patrolled left field for the Red Sox. Greenwell had the job throughout the nineties and drew comparisons with Yastrzemski for his left-handed bat and his ability to play the Green Monster.

Greenie is another rarity, a guy who played his entire career in Boston, 12 seasons, and finished as a lifetime .303 hitter with 130 home runs. His big breakthrough year came in 1988, his second full season with the Sox, when he hit 22 home runs, was third in the league in batting with a .325 average and third in RBIs with 119, and finished second to Jose Canseco of Oakland in the Most Valuable Player voting.

Unfortunately, although he continued to be a productive player for the Red Sox, Greenwell never matched those 1988 numbers in any category.

He didn't have quite the power numbers of his predecessors in left field, but Mike Greenwell was a career .300 hitter for more than 10 seasons in Boston.

Statistical Summaries

All statistics are for player's Red Sox career only.

HITTING

G = Games

H = Hits

HR = Home runs

RBI = Runs batted in

SB = Stolen bases

BA = Batting average

Left Fielder	Years	G	H	HR	RBI	SB	BA
Ted Williams *Hit three home runs in a game twice in 1957 (May 8, June 13)*	1939–42, 1946–60	2,292	2,654	521	1,839	24	.344
Carl Yastrzemski *Didn't commit an error all season (140 games) in outfield in 1977*	1961–83	3,308	3,419	452	1,844	168	.285
Manny Ramirez *Led majors with 25 intentional walks in 2001*	2001–03	416	499	111	336	3	.325

(continued)	Years	G	H	HR	RBI	SB	BA
Jim Rice *Hit 20 or more homers 11 times and had 100 or more RBI 8 times*	1974–89	2,089	2,452	373	1,451	58	.298
Mike Greenwell *Drove in all nine Sox runs on September 2, 1996, a record for a player driving in all his team's runs in one game.*	1985–96	1,269	1,400	130	726	80	.303

FIELDING

PO = Put-outs

A = Assists

E = Errors

DP = Double plays

TC/G = Total chances divided by games played

FA = Fielding average

Left Fielder	PO	A	E	DP	TC/G	FA
Ted Williams	4,158	140	113	30	2.1	.974
Carl Yastrzemski	3,941	195	82	30	2.0	.981
Manny Ramirez	416	18	9	1	1.7	.978
Jim Rice	3,103	137	66	19	2.1	.980
Mike Greenwell	2,091	85	42	15	1.9	.981

SEVEN

Center Fielder

Tᴴɪꜱ ɪꜱ ᴏɴᴇ ᴏꜰ ᴛʜᴇ ᴘᴏꜱɪᴛɪᴏɴꜱ where I must get personal and put at the top of the list **Dominic DiMaggio**, my contemporary, my teammate, and, to this day, one of my dearest friends. Some people may wonder how I can choose Dominic over Tris Speaker, a Hall of Famer, or even Fred Lynn, who won an American League Rookie of the Year Award and the Most Valuable Player Award both in the same year. But I don't think I need to apologize for calling Dom DiMaggio the greatest center fielder in Red Sox history.

Dominic should be in the Hall of Fame. To me, he was the perfect player. That man never made a mistake. He could hit, he could field, and he could run. He was a great base runner, a very intelligent player. He never missed a sign. He never made a bad throw, and he had an easy ball to handle. I don't think anybody could ever criticize him as a ballplayer. He had no minuses, only pluses. Why he's not in the Hall of Fame is beyond me. It breaks my heart. He's better than a lot of guys that are in there.

1. Dᴏᴍɪɴɪᴄ DɪMᴀɢɢɪᴏ

2. Tʀɪꜱ Sᴘᴇᴀᴋᴇʀ

3. Fʀᴇᴅ Lʏɴɴ

4. Eʟʟɪꜱ Bᴜʀᴋꜱ

5. Jɪᴍᴍʏ Pɪᴇʀꜱᴀʟʟ

Sure, he's been one of my dearest friends for more than 60 years, but I don't think I have to make any apologies for naming Dominic DiMaggio (left) as the greatest center fielder in Red Sox history. Here "the Little Professor" is shown with Washington's Mickey Vernon (center) and teammate Ted Williams at the 1946 All-Star break, when they were the three leading hitters in the league.

Maybe it's simply a case of Dominic being overshadowed by Ted Williams in Boston and by his own brother in New York.

Was he a better defensive center fielder than Joe? I think so, but when you see a guy every day, you come to appreciate the little things he does. He seemed to track balls as quickly as anybody. Comparing Dominic to Joe is like comparing a good little man to a good big man in boxing. The big man is always going to have the edge. You might say that, pound for pound, Dominic was the best center fielder ever.

Joe was 6′2″, 195 pounds. Dominic is 5′9″, 165, and he was one of the few baseball players who wore glasses in the field. They called him "the Little Professor" because with his glasses, he looked like a college professor. Still does. He had the same style and grace as Joe and the same class and dignity, on the field and off.

Dominic arrived in Boston in 1940, two years before I got there. He spent eleven years with the Red Sox, minus three years in the military, and he had 1,680 hits, scored 1,046 runs, and had a lifetime batting average of .298. Throw out his final year, 1953, when he retired after coming to bat only three times, and Dom averaged 168 hits and 105 runs a year for his career.

The reason Dominic retired was that he wasn't playing. The Red Sox had made Lou Boudreau the manager in 1952, and he decided he was going to go with a youth movement. On Opening Day, sitting in the dugout were Walt Dropo, Gene Stephens, Dominic, and I—all regulars the year before. On June 3, Dropo and I were traded to Detroit for George Kell, Dizzy Trout, Johnny Lipon, and Hoot Evers. Dominic got his job back and batted .294, but the next year, Boudreau put Tommy Umphlett in center field, and Dom was back on the bench. He couldn't stand not playing, so he quit. He was only 36.

When he left baseball, Dominic went into business. He started his own manufacturing company and was very successful. From time to time, Dominic would invite me to work for him, but that wasn't for me. I'm a baseball lifer.

Many people forget that in 1949, eight years after his brother set the major league record by hitting in 56 consecutive games, Dom set a Red Sox record that still stands by hitting in 34 straight games.

Although he was a great competitor and wanted to beat the Yankees in those years when we were always battling them for the pennant, Dom was very proud of his big brother. When Joe was on his hitting streak and the

Red Sox were playing at home, every day Ted Williams would talk to the operator of the left-field scoreboard in Fenway Park who had a radio and would keep Ted informed of what was going on around the American League. If Joe got a hit to extend his streak, Ted would yell over to center field, "Hey, Dommie, Joe just got one."

When I joined the Red Sox in 1942, Dom was leading off and I batted second, and we hit it off right away and worked well together. I could hit and run with him; I could bunt and run with him. Right after the war, we had one stretch where we worked the bunt-and-run every day. If Dominic got on base, he'd take a quick look at me and I'd rub my nose, a sign that I was going to bunt. I'd lay it down toward third so the third baseman would have to field it and leave third base unprotected. Dominic would take off and keep right on running all the way to third base.

We did that four or five days in a row, and it got in the newspapers. We went to Yankee Stadium for a series with the Yankees. Bill Dickey was catching. Dom got on base, and I gave him the sign that I was going to bunt. Dom took off and I put down a perfect bunt toward third. The third baseman—it was either Bobby Brown or Billy Johnson—came in and fielded it and threw me out at first, leaving third base unguarded. But the moment I squared away, Dickey took off from behind the plate and ran to third.

Dom headed for third, and there was Dickey waiting for him with the ball after taking the throw from the first baseman. He tagged Dom out and Dom said, "What are you doing here?"

"Gotcha," Dickey said. "I read the papers, too."

Dominic was also a key figure in my most embarrassing moment in baseball. You probably know I'm talking about the seventh game of the 1946 World Series against the Cardinals and Enos Slaughter's mad dash for home.

The game was in St. Louis, and we went into the eighth inning trailing 3–1, down to our last six outs. But Rip Russell, pinch hitting for Charlie Wagner, led off with a single, and George Metkovich, batting for Joe Dobson, doubled to put runners on second and third with nobody out. Eddie Dyer, the Cardinals' manager, went to the mound and took out Murry Dickson and brought in Harry Brecheen, the little left-hander they called "the Cat," who had won two games in the Series already.

Brecheen struck out Wally Moses, and I hit a line drive to right field, not deep enough to score Russell from third. DiMaggio came up with two outs and runners still on second and third. With Ted Williams on deck, Dominic knew Brecheen didn't want to walk him, so he waited for his pitch and got into it and drove it off the right-field wall. Russell and Metkovich scored to tie the game, 3–3, and Dom pulled into second with a double. But as he did, he pulled a hamstring and had to come out of the game, which turned out to be the key play of the Series.

Leon Culberson ran for Dominic and took over for him in center field in the bottom of the eighth. With two outs, Slaughter was on first and Harry Walker was the batter. "Harry the Hat" was a slap hitter who sprayed the ball to all fields. As Slaughter took off—he was stealing second—Walker hit a looping line drive to left-center.

Slaughter never stopped running. He headed for third and ran right through the stop sign of third-base coach Mike Gonzalez and raced home. I was covering second base because Slaughter was stealing. Then when the ball was hit, I had to go out and be the cutoff man. Culberson threw me a lollipop, and by the time I threw home, Slaughter had scored; that was the winning run that cost us the Series.

If Dominic had been in center field, it never would have happened. In fact, Dom has been quoted as saying, "If I was there, Slaughter wouldn't have scored—and he knows it."

I believe that. For one thing, Culberson was playing Walker a few steps toward right field, and Walker was a left-field hitter. Dom was an everyday center fielder who studied hitters and knew how to position himself. He probably would have been shading Walker toward left. And he certainly would have given me a better throw than I got from Culberson.

I'm not making excuses. I got the blame for that, and I accepted it. They said I hesitated and held the ball while Slaughter scored. The fact is none of that would have happened if Dom was in center field. That run would not have scored, and we might have won the World Series, so it became just another disappointment in a long line of Red Sox disappointments.

For a while, I was sensitive about the criticism I got for that play, but I learned to get over it.

After the Series, I went home to Portland, and one Saturday I went with a group of buddies to the Oregon–Oregon State football game in Corvallis. It was a rainy day. I mean really pouring. Oregon State kicked off, and the Oregon player fumbled the ball, and it was recovered by Oregon State. This guy sitting a few rows behind me yells, "Give the ball to Pesky, he'll hold on to it."

Even I had to laugh.

Tris Speaker played his first major league game 12 years before I was born and his last major league game while I was in grade school, so I obviously never saw him play. But I read enough about him and heard enough about him to know he belongs on my list of all-time Red Sox center fielders. For example, he was the seventh player inducted into the Hall of Fame; he had a lifetime batting average for 22 seasons of .345, seventh highest in baseball history; had more than 3,500 hits; and holds the all-time career record for doubles with 792.

Though I was never fortunate enough to see him play, many folks believe Tris Speaker was the greatest center fielder of all time.

The reason I put him behind Dom DiMaggio among Red Sox center fielders—besides my personal prejudice for Dominic—is that Speaker had his greatest years in Cleveland. He played for the Red Sox for nine seasons and batted over .300 seven times, including a high of .383 (third in the league behind Ty Cobb's .410 and "Shoeless" Joe Jackson's .395) in 1912.

Speaker started out with Boston in 1907, the year the team became known as the "Red Sox," but he was sent back to the minor leagues for failing to hit. It wasn't until two years later that he broke into the Red Sox outfield and made his mark. In 1915, he helped the Red Sox win their third World Series, but his average had been steadily slipping, from .383 to .363 to .338 to .322, and the team owner, Joe Lannin, threatened to cut his salary to less than $10,000.

When Speaker refused to budge, Lannin traded him to the Indians for two players and $55,000. I have a feeling the money was more important to Lannin than the two players. This deal came down four years before another Boston owner, Harry Frazee, sold Babe Ruth to the Yankees, leaving frustrated Red Sox fans to wonder how many championships their team might have won with an outfield that had Babe Ruth in right and Tris Speaker in center.

In his first season in Cleveland, Speaker won his only batting title with a .386 average and would bat .354 in 11 seasons with the Indians.

Never having seen him play, I have no idea how good Speaker was defensively, but he has the reputation of possibly being the greatest center fielder ever. His plaque in Cooperstown reads, "greatest center fielder of his day."

They say he played a very shallow center field and took many hits away from opposing batters. I know he played in the so-called dead-ball era, but his defensive numbers can't be ignored. He's the all-time leader in outfield assists (448) and double plays (135). One statistic in particular jumps out at me. In a six-year period from 1910 through 1915, Speaker recorded 161 assists, an average of almost 27 assists a year. That's unbelievable. Today, if an outfielder gets 15 assists, it's a lot.

I don't know if the scoring rules were different in Speaker's day or if playing so shallow he got many of his assists by forcing runners at second on base hits. What I do know is that 27 assists a season for six seasons is an awesome number. It couldn't happen today.

*H*is zany antics on the field, his penchant for speaking his mind and letting the chips fall where they may, a book and movie about his life detailing a nervous breakdown that interrupted a promising career and left him stigmatized by the baseball community, and a career batting average of .272 with only 104 home runs in 17 seasons cloud the fact that Jimmy Piersall was regarded as a truly great center fielder, hailed by many as the greatest ever.

Piersall took over the Red Sox center-field position from Boston favorite Dominic DiMaggio in 1954 and was soon hailed as a worthy successor to the Little Professor. Renowned for playing the shallowest center field in the major leagues, Piersall could go get 'em with the best, and he won two Gold Gloves with the Red Sox. His best seasons at the plate came in 1956 and 1957, when he hit 67 doubles, 11 triples, and 33 home runs; drove in 150 runs; and scored 194.

He never again reached those heights with the bat, although he had his moments. And it was his wacky behavior on the field, and behind a microphone, that became his legacy.

While playing for the expansion New York Mets in 1963, Piersall hit the 100th home run of his career in the old Polo Grounds and celebrated the occasion by circling the bases backward, which astonished even his manager, Casey Stengel, himself known for his strange verbiage as well as his weird behavior on the field (while playing for the Brooklyn Dodgers, Stengel once doffed his cap and a bird flew out).

Playing for Cleveland, Piersall once hid behind the center-field monuments in Yankee Stadium. Pitcher Jim Kaat remembered another Piersall antic when Piersall was playing for the Angels.

"The fans were getting on him unmercifully, as they always did," Kaat recalled. "There were two outs in the ninth, and the Angels were winning the game when a fly ball was hit to center field. Piersall turned around to face the fans who had been getting on him, gestured to them, then turned around and caught the ball for the final out of the game."

Piersall became a national celebrity because of his book, *Fear Strikes Out*, which was made into a movie starring Anthony Perkins as Jimmy. In it, Piersall recounted the enormous pressure to succeed that was instilled in him by his father. Ultimately, it caused Piersall's mental breakdown and subsequent hospitalization to treat the condition.

When he was released and returned to baseball, Piersall became the unhappy target of fans who bombarded him with taunts and insults in cities all around the major leagues. "Crazy" was one of the kinder epithets hurled at him, to which Piersall responded with good humor.

"I've got papers that say I'm sane," he said. "Where's yours?"

When he retired as a player, Piersall wound up broadcasting games for the Chicago White Sox and continued to be outspoken and controversial on the air. He called them as he saw them, sparing no feelings, pulling no punches. He even criticized White Sox management, which was tantamount to biting the hand that fed him, with the expected result. He was fired.

The way he started out, **Fred Lynn** looked as if he would end up in the Hall of Fame and rival Ted Williams as the Red Sox's greatest player. He might have, too, if he hadn't broken down physically and if he hadn't forced the Red Sox to trade him to California, his home.

Lynn had one of the greatest rookie seasons ever in 1975. He batted .331, hit 21 home runs, drove in 105 runs, led the league in doubles and runs scored, and made some of the greatest catches you'd ever want to see in center field. In one game in Detroit, he hit three home runs, drove in 10 runs, and had 16 total bases. He was named the American League Rookie of the Year *and* the Most Valuable Player. That had never happened before, and it wouldn't happen again until Ichiro Suzuki of Seattle did it in 2001.

Four years after his great rookie season, Freddy again led the league in hitting with a .333 average. In six seasons in Boston, Lynn batted under .300 just twice. But he longed to play in California, where he grew up, and the Red Sox accommodated him by trading him to the Angels in 1981 for Frank Tanana and Joe Rudi.

After he was traded, Lynn was still a top-flight player, but he never was the ballplayer he had been in Boston, when he looked like a certain future Hall of Famer. Maybe it was because he missed hitting in Fenway Park. More likely, it was because of a series of injuries, many of them coming as a result of his aggressive style of play.

Most of us in Boston strongly believe that Fred Lynn would be in the Hall of Fame if he'd stayed with the Red Sox. Here he is making one of his famous catches during the 1975 World Series, the year he won both Rookie of the Year and MVP honors.

After he was traded, Lynn was still a top-flight player, but he never was the ballplayer he had been in Boston, when he looked like a certain future Hall of Famer. Maybe it was because he missed hitting in Fenway Park. More likely, it was because of a series of injuries, many of them coming as a result of his aggressive style of play.

When I think of Fred Lynn, I just can't help wondering what he might have been if only he hadn't left Boston.

Ellis Burks is another player the Red Sox let get away (how many times have we heard that?). What a good-looking young player he was when he broke in with the Red Sox in 1987 at the age of 22. He had 20 home runs and stole 27 bases in his rookie season, only the third player in Red Sox history to go

20–20 in the same season. He could run, and he had great range in the field. He was a future star, but he stayed in Boston only six seasons.

Since then, he has played for four other teams and is closing in on a 20-year career. Because of injuries, he's no longer the defensive player he once was, and he has been used primarily as a DH in recent years. But he's still a productive hitter, and when he's finished, he will have had an outstanding career.

Ellis Burks broke in with the Sox and spent six great years in Boston; he's now closing in on a 20-year career with five teams.

Jimmy Piersall was definitely a character—and that's what people remember most about him—but he was also one of the finest defensive center fielders of all time.

Simply playing center field, **Jim Piersall** is as good as I've ever seen, right up there with the DiMaggios, Willie Mays, Paul Blair, Ken Griffey Jr., Fred Lynn, and any other center fielder you can name. Like so many great center fielders, Jimmy played very shallow, which allowed him to cut off a lot of hits.

Unfortunately, his bat prevented him from being a perennial All-Star. He batted only .272 for his career and had only 104 home runs and 591 RBIs in a 17-year career.

It's also a shame that Piersall is remembered less for his fielding ability than for the movie of his life, *Fear Strikes Out*, with Anthony Perkins playing Jimmy, and for his zany antics like hiding behind the center-field monuments in Yankee Stadium when he was with the Indians and running around the bases backward when he hit his 100th career home run while with the Mets in 1963.

I haven't included Johnny Damon on my list because he has been with the Red Sox such a short time. But he has made an impact in his first two seasons in Boston and has impressed me as a hitter and a fielder and with his aggressive style of play. Give him a few more years, and he will be pushing his way onto my list of the top five Red Sox center fielders.

Statistical Summaries

All statistics are for player's Red Sox career only.

HITTING

G = Games

H = Hits

HR = Home runs

RBI = Runs batted in

SB = Stolen bases

BA = Batting average

Center Fielder	Years	G	H	HR	RBI	SB	BA
Dominic DiMaggio *Scored more than 100 runs seven times*	1940–42, 1946–53	1,399	1,680	87	618	100	.298
Tris Speaker *Holds major league record for most career double plays by out-fielder, 135*	1907–15	1,065	1,327	39	542	267	.337
Fred Lynn *Shares A.L. record of four All-Star Game home runs with Ted Williams*	1974–80	828	944	124	521	43	.308

(continued)	Years	G	H	HR	RBI	SB	BA
Ellis Burks *Hit two home runs in one inning on August 27, 1990*	1987–92	722	785	93	387	93	.281
Jim Piersall *Best career fielding average of any Red Sox outfielder (.989)*	1950, 1952–58	931	919	66	366	58	.273

FIELDING

PO = Put-outs

A = Assists

E = Errors

DP = Double plays

TC/G = Total chances divided by games played

FA = Fielding average

Center Fielder	PO	A	E	DP	TC/G	FA
Dominic DiMaggio	3,859	147	89	32	3.0	.978
Tris Speaker	2,562	207	109	64	2.7	.962
Fred Lynn	2,213	65	29	16	2.8	.987
Ellis Burks	1,662	43	25	6	2.5	.986
Jim Piersall	2,239	65	25	14	2.6	.989

EIGHT

Right Fielder

I'M WELL AWARE THAT **Carl Yastrzemski**'s primary position was left field and his secondary position was first base and that he played only a few games in right field. Nevertheless, I'm pulling rank here, exercising my managerial privilege, and making Yaz the number one right fielder on my all-time Red Sox team. Hey, it's my team. I can do with it what I want.

How can you have an all-time Red Sox team in which Yastrzemski is not in the starting lineup somewhere? Outside of Ted Williams, he's the greatest Red Sox player ever, number two in the minds and hearts of Red Sox fans, and it's no disgrace to be number two when number one is Williams.

Because of free agency, interleague trading, multimillion-dollar salaries, and the luxury tax imposed on teams' payrolls, today's players, even the great ones, rarely play their entire careers with one team. Yaz did—all 23 seasons in Boston. That makes him a dinosaur.

1. CARL YASTRZEMSKI

2. DWIGHT EVANS

3. TONY CONIGLIARO

4. REGGIE SMITH

5. JACKIE JENSEN

In those 23 seasons, Yaz had 3,419 hits, won three batting titles, hit almost 500 home runs, drove in more than 1,800 runs, was the last player to win the

Triple Crown (1967), played in two World Series, and was elected to the Hall of Fame. When he retired, he had played in more games (3,308) than any other player in history (and is still first among American Leaguers), and he is the only American Leaguer with 3,000 hits and 400 home runs.

Yastrzemski was a guy that wore on you. He wasn't very big, just 5′11″ and 175 pounds in his prime, but he was strong and a tough kid and a gamer. He could run and he could throw. And he could hit.

Yastrzemski was a guy that wore on you. He wasn't very big, just 5′11″ and 175 pounds in his prime, but he was strong and a tough kid and a gamer. He could run and he could throw. And he could hit. He carried the team when the Red Sox won the pennant in 1967, the first time in 21 years they had won a pennant.

I talked earlier about how he moved to first base to make room for Jim Rice, which was only the sensible thing to do, and became an outstanding first baseman. He also played a few seasons as the Red Sox's regular center fielder. Carl was the longtime captain of the Red Sox and the ultimate team player.

98

How could you have an all-time Red Sox team without having Yaz in the starting lineup? I'm pulling rank and making him my number one right fielder.

Dwight Evans was as good a defensive right fielder as there has ever been, and later in his career he blossomed into one of the game's better hitters.

I don't mean to slight **Dwight Evans**, who was as good a right fielder as I've ever seen. He was clearly the best right fielder in the American League in his time, right up there with Al Kaline, Rocky Colavito, Roger Maris, and any other American League right fielder you can name. If I didn't feel I had to find a starting spot for Carl Yastrzemski on my all-time team, Evans would be my number one right fielder.

Yaz is the only player to have appeared in more games as a Red Sox player than Evans. In his 19 seasons with the Red Sox, Evans won eight Gold Gloves for defense. Willie Mays, Roberto Clemente, and Kaline are the only outfielders who had won more at the time.

For 13 seasons, from 1972 through 1984, Ken Singleton and Dwight Evans were contemporaries and rivals, among the premier right fielders in the American League, Singleton with the Baltimore Orioles, and Evans with the Boston Red Sox.

In a distinguished 15-year career, Singleton batted .282, 10 points higher than his Boston counterpart, but Evans, with longevity (19 years a member of the Red Sox and a final season with the Orioles), hit 385 home runs to Singleton's 246, had 1,384 RBIs to Singleton's 1,065, and was the defensive standard by which all right fielders were measured.

"Going back to the seventies and eighties, Dwight Evans was no doubt the best fielding right fielder in the league," said Singleton. "He had 385 career home runs; that's quite a few, but people remember him for his eight Gold Gloves, his great plays, the great catch he made against Joe Morgan in the 1975 World Series. He had a great throwing arm, he positioned himself well, but with all the big hitters the Red Sox had, he was overshadowed offensively while he might have stood out on other teams.

"I can't remember Evans making any great play against me, but I always knew he was out there, and he always seemed to make a great play against our team.

"I didn't have the skills Dwight Evans had as a right fielder. I had a good arm, but I was a more stationary right fielder. Evans covered a lot of ground. He was a right fielder who was capable of playing center field if the Red Sox needed him there. I was a right fielder who [Orioles' manager] Earl Weaver just hoped the ball was hit in my direction and I didn't have to go too far to get it.

"Evans played the type of right field that I wished I could play. I liked to watch him, to watch what he was doing out there. I was just in awe of him in right field and the Gold Gloves he won, and deservedly so."

Another right fielder of the day, Lou Piniella of the Yankees, remembered Evans as "an all-around solid player who never got the total recognition that he should have. The Red Sox had [Jim] Rice while Evans was there; they had

Fred Lynn, Yaz, Big George Scott, Carlton Fisk, and Rick Burleson. Basically, the Red Sox had an All-Star team on the field in those years. They had great talent.

"Evans played right field so well. He had a great throwing arm. And he developed into a damn good major league hitter where he could hit the ball with power and hit .300 and drive in runs. He had an outstanding career. You don't hear much about him, but he was a mainstay as far as playing every day, playing hard, and helping to win ballgames. He was a tough out, and if he had played on other teams, he would have gotten more recognition."

People who followed the Red Sox, and the American League, knew all about Evans' defense—how he mastered the tricky right-field corner in Fenway Park and the cannon he had for an arm. Then, in the 1975 World Series, the whole country got to see what we all knew about him when he robbed Joe Morgan of a game-winning home run with a leaping catch in the eleventh inning of Game 6 and then turned it into a double play. That was the game the Red Sox won on Carlton Fisk's dramatic home run in the bottom of the twelfth. It was the most famous home run in Red Sox history, but it wouldn't have happened if it weren't for Evans' catch.

Evans was so good defensively that the Red Sox kept him in right field early in his career when he wasn't much of a run producer at bat. Later in his career, when he learned to be more selective at the plate, his offense picked up and caught up with his defense. He led the league in walks three times, and as the walks mounted, so did the home runs and RBIs. In a six-year span, from 1984 to 1989, Evans averaged 27 homers, 102 RBIs, and 95 walks per year.

Tony Conigliaro was one of the tragedies of this game. He was the best-looking young ballplayer I ever saw. Big—6'3"—good-looking, a local kid from Revere, and a right-handed hitter in Fenway Park who could run and throw and hit with power. He had it all.

He came to us in 1964 when I was the manager. He had played only 50 games of minor league baseball, in the New York–Penn League, a short-season, Class A league. I had never seen him play when he came to spring training. What I did in exhibition games was take out the veteran players in

101

the latter part of the game so I could take a look at some of our young players, like Dalton Jones, Russ Gibson, Rico Petrocelli, and Tony Conigliaro.

Conigliaro was only 19, but he showed me so much in spring training that I kept him, and he batted .290 in his rookie year and hit 24 home runs although his season was cut short in August when he broke his arm.

The next year, he hit 32 homers; at 20, he was the youngest player to lead the American League in home runs. Now he was a star, with his whole career ahead of him. But in August of 1967, Tony C. was hit in the face with a pitch, and it broke his cheekbone. The beaning affected his eyesight, and he missed the entire 1968 season, but he came back in 1969 and, in 1970, he hit 36 home runs.

He was never the same after the broken cheekbone. His vision was still impaired. After the 1970 season, he was traded to the Angels. He still suffered from poor vision, and he retired in July of 1971.

He sat out three years and then tried a comeback with the Red Sox in 1975. He played in only 21 games and hit a couple of home runs, but he was hitting under .200, so he quit for good.

102

Tony Conigliaro played all three outfield positions well, but he makes my all-time team in right field.

The supremely talented and versatile Reggie Smith won a Gold Glove in center field for the Sox, but later moved to right.

That wasn't the end of the tragedy of Tony C. Seven years later, riding in a car with his brother, Billy, who also played for the Red Sox, Tony suffered a heart attack that left him in bad shape. He passed away in 1990. He was only 45.

It's one of the saddest stories ever in baseball. Here was a player who had such natural gifts, he could have been one of the all-time greats if he had just a little luck.

Reggie Smith, like Yaz and Tony C., is another player you could put in any of the three outfield positions. He was the Sox's center fielder as a rookie when they won the pennant in 1967 and in 1968 when he won a Gold Glove and led the league in putouts. Later, he moved to right.

Jackie Jensen might not have lived up to his potential, but he still had a great career with the Sox and was the league MVP in 1958.

Reggie batted over .300 three times and hit more than 20 home runs in five straight seasons with the Red Sox. In 1974, he was traded to the Cardinals for pitcher Rick Wise.

Reggie Smith was the first switch-hitter to hit 100 home runs in both the National and American League and the first switch-hitter to hit 2 home runs in the same game twice in each league.

Jackie Jensen had all the tools to be a big star in baseball, and he had all the attributes to be a big fan favorite and a media darling. He was your typical California golden boy with curly blond hair, a surfer's body, and a famous, athletic wife (Olympic diving champion Zoe Ann Olsen). And he had been an All-American running back at the University of California.

When he came up to the Yankees in 1950, it was with the reputation that he would be the one to succeed Joe DiMaggio as their big hitter. He was rated slightly ahead of Mickey Mantle, and he arrived in New York a year before Mantle did.

After two mediocre seasons by Jensen—and the enormous potential Mantle showed in his first season—the Yankees decided to cast their lot with the Mick as DiMaggio's heir, and they traded Jensen to Washington. A year later, he was traded again, to the Red Sox.

Jensen spent seven seasons in Boston and had a very successful career with the Red Sox, although not as successful as had been predicted of him and nowhere near the success Mantle had in New York. Jensen was a three-time All-Star and the Most Valuable Player in the American League in 1958. He led the league in runs batted in three times, and Ted Williams once called Jensen "the best outfielder I ever saw."

Jensen played 11 seasons in the major leagues. He could have played longer and had an even more productive career, but by the late fifties and early sixties, major league teams were beginning to fly a lot more than they had, and Jensen had a morbid fear of flying. Because he couldn't overcome that fear, he retired after the 1961 season.

Another disclaimer here: baseball historians are going to wonder why the name Harry Hooper doesn't appear on my list. He was a Hall of Famer and the Red Sox right fielder for 12 seasons and four pennant winners. But that was from 1909 to 1920, long before my time. I know very little about him, and I don't know anybody who saw him play, so I'll abstain from selecting him for my list except to say he probably belongs in there somewhere.

Statistical Summaries

All statistics are for player's Red Sox career only.

HITTING

G = Games

H = Hits

HR = Home runs

RBI = Runs batted in

SB = Stolen bases

BA = Batting average

Right Fielder	Years	G	H	HR	RBI	SB	BA
Carl Yastrzemski *Led league in outfield assists a major league record seven times*	1961–83	3,308	3,419	452	1,844	168	.285
Dwight Evans *Career World Series average of .300 with three home runs and 14 RBIs in 14 games*	1972–90	2,505	2,373	379	1,346	76	.272
Tony Conigliaro *Combined with brother Billy to homer in the same game twice in 1970*	1964–67, 1969–71, 1975	802	790	162	501	17	.267

(continued)	Years	G	H	HR	RBI	SB	BA
Reggie Smith *Led A.L. in doubles twice (1968, 1971)*	1966–73	1,014	1,058	149	536	84	.281
Jackie Jensen *Drove in 100 or more runs five times in his seven seasons with Red Sox*	1954–59, 1961	1,039	929	170	733	95	.283

FIELDING

PO = Put-outs

A = Assists

E = Errors

DP = Double plays

TC/G = Total chances divided by games played

FA = Fielding average

Right Fielder	PO	A	E	DP	TC/G	FA
Carl Yastrzemski	3,941	195	82	30	2.0	.981
Dwight Evans	4,255	151	57	40	2.1	.987
Tony Conigliaro	1,328	42	32	6	1.8	.977
Reggie Smith	2,332	72	60	11	2.5	.976
Jackie Jensen	2,032	92	51	18	2.1	.977

NINE

Right-Handed Pitcher

Cy Young, who many baseball experts say is the greatest pitcher the game has known, won more games than any other pitcher in baseball history, by far. He won some 200 games more than **Roger Clemens**. And yet, I'm picking Clemens as the best pitcher in Red Sox history. In fact, I'll go even further and say that "the Rocket" is the greatest pitcher I ever saw.

Of course, I never saw Cy Young pitch. His last season was eight years before I was born. But I have record books with which to compare Clemens and Young.

Remember, I'm judging players only by their years with the Red Sox. Young spent eight seasons in Boston, from 1901 to 1908. Clemens was there for 13 seasons, from 1984 through 1996. In comparing their records when they were with the Red Sox, I came up with some astonishing similarities.

1. Roger Clemens

2. Cy Young

3. Pedro Martinez

4. Luis Clemente Tiant

5. Tex Hughson

They won exactly the same number of games, 192, the most by any Red Sox pitcher. Clemens lost 111 games; Young lost 112, also the most for a Red Sox pitcher. They both had 38 shutouts. Clemens, with four-and-a-half more years in Boston, started more games, 382 to 327. Young completed more, 275 to 100, which was a sign of the times, not a commentary on Clemens' failing. In the days that Young was pitching, there was no such thing as relief pitchers as we now know them. Back then, pitchers were expected to finish what they started. They usually pitched with two or three days' rest, and often in relief between starts. For example, Cy Young pitched in relief 30 times in his eight years with the Red Sox and won 12 of those games. In his 13 seasons in Boston, Clemens pitched in relief just once.

The one area that sets Clemens apart from Young is strikeouts. In his 13 seasons with the Red Sox, Roger struck out 2,590 batters. In eight seasons in Boston, Young had only 1,341 strikeouts. With the Red Sox, Rocket had 68 games of 10 or more strikeouts; Young had 8 such games. When he was in Boston, Clemens led the league in strikeouts three times; Young did it only once. Of his 13 seasons in Boston, Clemens had 200 or more strikeouts eight times; Young struck out 200 or more batters twice in his 8 seasons in Boston. Clemens also had two games with the Red Sox in which he struck out 20 batters. Young never came close.

And one more thing: Roger won three Cy Young Awards in Boston. Cy Young never won the Cy Young Award. He never even won the Roger Clemens Award.

In my years in baseball, I've had the privilege of seeing some great pitchers—hard throwers like Bob Feller, Virgil Trucks, Allie Reynolds, Vic Raschi, Dizzy Trout, and Bob Lemon. Roger Clemens is the best I've ever seen. It's amazing what he has been able to accomplish past his 40th birthday. Only Nolan Ryan is in a class with Clemens as a dominant power pitcher past the age of 40.

One of the worst decisions in Red Sox history (almost up there with letting Babe Ruth go) was when the Sox failed to re-sign Clemens after the 1996 season. He had a record of 10–13, his fourth straight mediocre season. He was 34 and his contract was up. But he had led the league with 257 strikeouts, so it should have been obvious there was nothing wrong with his arm. And if Roger still had arm strength, there was really no reason to believe he was finished, even at the age of 34.

The Red Sox offered him a contract that was far below the $5.5 million he had made in his final year in Boston, and Roger was insulted by the offer.

Clemens is a man of enormous pride, and he always was one of the hardest workers on the team. He was a physical fitness fanatic, a guy who worked tirelessly to improve. When I was a coach, Roger was having trouble

Roger Clemens has to be considered the best pitcher in Red Sox history—though Sox fans cringe when they look at all he's accomplished after leaving Boston.

throwing to bases on balls hit back to the mound. He had a vigorous follow-through and was usually out of position to field and throw after he delivered the pitch. One of my assignments was to take him out to center field and hit ground balls back at him and have him practice fielding the ball and throwing to the bases. We did that on days when he wasn't scheduled to pitch. He worked so hard until he not only improved his throwing to the bases, he improved his fielding and became a better-than-average fielder.

The Red Sox refused to budge on their offer, and Dan Duquette, the general manager, made some comments that Clemens was on the downside of his career. Knowing Roger, those remarks no doubt motivated him to get himself in the best shape of his life. He signed a free-agent contract with Toronto and then later was traded to the Yankees, which really burned Red Sox fans.

Many consider Cy Young to be the best pitcher in both Red Sox history and baseball history, though he obviously doesn't come close to Clemens' six Cy Young Awards.

Since he left Boston, Roger has won more than 100 games, had three 20-win seasons, won three more Cy Youngs, won his 300th game, led the league in strikeouts twice, and has moved into third place on the all-time strikeout list.

Not bad for a guy who was thought to be over-the-hill almost a decade ago.

The case for **Cy Young** as the number two pitcher in Red Sox history has already been made, in the comparison with Clemens and with so little to differentiate the two. The totality of Young's career (11H seasons in Cleveland, 8 with the Red Sox, 2 in St. Louis, and a half season with the Boston Braves to finish his career) is staggering—first all-time in wins (511), losses (316), complete games (749), and innings pitched (7,356)—all records that will never be broken because of the way the game has changed and the way pitchers are pampered these days.

That body of work is why, in 1956, when they instituted an award for the best pitcher in baseball, they called it the Cy Young Award.

On most teams, with what he accomplished in only his first six years in Boston, **Pedro Martinez** would be the franchise's number one pitcher. Going up against Roger Clemens and Cy Young makes it difficult to rate Pedro any higher than third best. (Imagine building a pitching staff and having Pedro as your number three starter.)

To me, Martinez is the best pitcher in the game today. His only drawback is his lack of durability. Because of his size—only 5'11", 170 pounds—and because he puts so much effort into every pitch, Pedro pretty much has to be babied by the Red Sox, who can't afford to lose him. So he rarely completes games, and he has missed time with shoulder problems.

But he's a tough little guy, a great competitor, and a very intelligent pitcher. When he's sound, he overpowers hitters with his stuff. He also baffles them with the best change-up in the game. He's a master at setting up hitters and finishing them off. He can put you away with four different pitches.

He [Pedro Martinez] is a tough little guy, a great competitor, and a very intelligent pitcher. When he's sound, he overpowers hitters with his stuff. He also baffles them with the best change-up in the game. He's a master at setting up hitters and finishing them off. He can put you away with four different pitches.

They were teammates briefly in 1986, a couple of 300-game winners on opposite ends of their careers. Tom Seaver, 41 years old, had already joined the exclusive 300-win club when he was traded to Boston in June. He won five games for the Red Sox (he would finish his career with 311 victories), which was almost exactly their margin of victory over the Yankees in the American League East.

That 1986 season would be 23-year-old Roger Clemens' breakout year. He had won only 16 games in his first two seasons, but he put together a brilliant 24–4 record with a 2.48 earned run average and 238 strikeouts to win his first Cy Young Award on his route to 300 wins.

"The biggest thing that I recognized about Clemens the first time I saw him," said Seaver, "is that he was on the front edge of greatness and what was starting to blossom was that killer instinct, that high level of competitiveness and being self-demanding. There was a self-expectation about him, which sometimes can be a double-edged sword. Success begins to feed your need for success and makes you hungrier. Roger had a terrific work ethic. Even then, he was a very hard worker."

Clemens continued to make demands on his body for another 20 years and remained a productive pitcher to the end, throwing his fastball in the high 90s at the age of 41. Only Nolan Ryan among power pitchers was able to do it for so long. The common denominator between Clemens and Ryan was their rigorous workout regimen.

It would have been interesting to be a fly on the wall when Clemens and Seaver, two pitching giants, talked as teammates in 1986, but that fly would have come away unfulfilled. There weren't a great many conversations about the art of pitching between them.

"We were in the middle of a pennant race," Seaver said, "and Roger was on his way to a Cy Young season. In a situation like that, everybody has his own routine. I wouldn't go to him to suggest something—I was an old curmudgeon at the time, in my 20th season—I let him come to me when he wanted to. He did come to me one time to ask me how I held my slider, but I didn't have a lot of conversations with him."

Of his time in Boston, Seaver said, "I loved it over there. It was close to my home in Connecticut, and it was such a great place to play. I loved playing for [manager] John McNamara. But I never got caught up in 'the Curse of the Bambino' thing. When you're a player, you don't get wrapped up in stuff like that. Maybe if I was there five or ten years I might have. But I was only there for two-and-a-half months."

Seaver's Red Sox days, and his career, came to an abrupt end when he tore a cartilage in his knee and was left off the Red Sox postseason roster.

What if Seaver had been eligible for the World Series? And what if McNamara had brought him out of the bullpen to pitch to Mookie Wilson? Would things have turned out differently? Who knows?

In six years, Martinez has cracked the Red Sox top 10 in wins, has passed Clemens in 10-strikeout games, is second to Clemens in strikeouts, and is first in winning percentage, having won almost 80 percent of his games in a Boston uniform. He also holds the Red Sox record for most strikeouts in a season with 313 in 1999.

There's little doubt that if he stays healthy, and if the Red Sox don't let him get away as they have with so many others, Martinez will move up on more Red Sox pitching lists. But considering his age and his small frame and previous physical limitations, it's unlikely he will ever surpass Clemens and Young as the top two pitchers in Red Sox history.

Number four on my list of Red Sox right-handed pitchers is one of my favorites and one of the most popular players ever to play in Boston, **Luis Clemente Tiant**, "el Tiante," whose name appears on the top 10 lists of most Red Sox pitching categories—fourth in wins, tied for seventh in 10-strikeout games, third in innings, fourth in shutouts, third in starts, seventh in complete games, fourth in strikeouts.

Tiant, whose dad was a great pitcher and a national hero in Cuba, came to the major leagues with the Indians in 1964 after spending five-and-a-half years in the minor leagues and was almost an instant star. He won 10 games his first year, pitched four consecutive shutouts in 1966, and won 21 games for Cleveland in 1968. He led the league in ERA (1.60) and shutouts (9) and

Hard to believe that with all that Pedro Martinez has accomplished, he has to take a back seat to not one but two other pitchers on this list. I don't think you could find three more formidable right-handers on any all-time staff throughout baseball history.

set a major league record (since broken) with 32 strikeouts in two consecutive starts, including 19 in a 10-inning game against the Twins.

But the following season, Luis lost 20 games (the Indians had forbidden him to play winter ball, which he had done every previous year, and that was believed to have affected him adversely). After the 1970 season, the Indians traded him and Stan Williams to Minnesota for four players, including Dean Chance and Graig Nettles.

Luis Tiant was on the verge of retiring when he came to Boston, where he was revitalized and now resides in all the team's pitching records.

In Minnesota, Tiant won his first six decisions and then suffered a hairline fracture in his shoulder that sidelined him for two months in the middle of the season. When he returned, he wasn't the same pitcher. He was released by the Twins at the end of spring training in 1971, hooked on with the Braves, and was released again after pitching five games for their Richmond farm team.

Tiant went looking for a job, and the Red Sox gave him one. They sent him to their Louisville farm team, where Darrell Johnson was managing, and DJ saved Looey's career. Tiant had begun to use what would become his trademark delivery—he'd twist and turn and swivel his hips so that his back

That's Tex Hughson in the middle, surrounded by (from left) Bobby Doerr, me, Dave Ferris, and our manager, Joe Cronin, at spring training in 1946.

was to the hitter, then he'd pivot and throw. He used so many different deliveries and release points, hitters never knew where the ball was coming from. He'd vary the speed on all his pitches so that it seemed he had 8 or 10 different pitches.

The Red Sox brought him to Boston late in the 1971 season, and he won only one of eight decisions. But the next year, he won 15 games and led the American League in earned run average. In the next four seasons, Tiant was one of the best pitchers in baseball and the ace of the Red Sox staff. From 1973 to 1976, he won 81 games, including three 20-win seasons, and became one of the most beloved players the Red Sox ever had, a team leader and a character with a wonderful sense of humor who spoke in a thick Cuban accent and seemed always to have a big cigar in his mouth, even in the shower.

Tiant became a free agent after the 1978 season and wound up, to the dismay of Red Sox fans, pitching for with the Yankees.

Eventually, Looey returned to Boston and is now a broadcaster of Red Sox games on Spanish radio and television.

Picking number five on my list of the top five right-handed pitchers in Red Sox history is no easy task because the Sox have had so many outstanding right-handed pitchers, like Ferguson Jenkins, Jesse Tannehill, Bill Dineen, Smokey Joe Wood, Dutch Leonard, Bullet Joe Bush, Carl Mays, Ernie Shore, Waite Hoyt, Sad Sam Jones, Howard Ehmke, Red Ruffing, Wes Ferrell, Jack Kramer, Frank Sullivan, Bill Monbouquette, Earl Wilson, Jim Lonborg, Tom Seaver, Juan Marichal, Jack Chesbro, and Joe Dobson.

Some of them I didn't see and don't feel qualified to judge. Others were with the Red Sox for too short a period of time to qualify. So I have narrowed the choice to two of my teammates, Tex Hughson and Dave "Boo" Ferris.

Ferris' career began spectacularly when he won 21 and 25 games in his first two seasons. But he won just 19 more games in a career that was shortened by asthma and arm problems. Therefore, my choice for number five on my list is **Tex Hughson**. Tex led the American League with 22 wins in 1942, my rookie season, and combined with Ferris to give us a great one-two punch when we won the pennant in 1946. Although Hughson won 20 games that season, to Ferris' 25, I give the nod to Tex because he won 96 games for the Sox in his career, 31 more than Ferris

Statistical Summaries

All statistics are for player's Red Sox career only.

PITCHING

G = Games
W = Games won
L = Games lost
PCT = Winning percentage
SV = Saves
SO = Strikeouts
ERA = Earned run average

Right-Handed Pitcher	Years	G	W	L	PCT	SHO	SO	ERA
Roger Clemens *Led A.L. in ERA three consecutive seasons from 1990–92*	1984–96	383	192	111	.634	38	2,590	3.06
Cy Young *Pitched first no-hitter (a perfect game) in Red Sox team history on May 5, 1904*	1901–08	327	192	112	.632	38	1,341	2.00

(continued)	Years	G	W	L	PCT	SHO	SO	ERA
Pedro Martinez *Achieved All-Star game record of four consecutive strikeouts at the start of the game in 1999*	1998–2003	170	101	28	.783	18	1,456	2.26
Luis Tiant *Went 3–0 in 1975 post-season (1–0 in ALCS; 2–0 in World Series)*	1971–78	274	122	81	.601	26	1,075	3.36
Tex Hughson *Led A.L. in wins, innings pitched, complete games, and strikeouts in 1942*	1941–44, 1946–59	225	96	54	.640	19	693	2.94

FIELDING

PO = Put-outs

A = Assists

E = Errors

DP = Double plays

TC/G = Total chances divided by games played

FA = Fielding average

Right-Handed Pitcher	PO	A	E	DP	TC/G	FA
Roger Clemens	214	275	15	12	1.3	.970
Cy Young	55	689	40	17	2.4	.949
Pedro Martinez	73	103	7	6	1.1	.962
Luis Tiant	109	187	15	14	1.1	.952
Tex Hughson	70	231	9	16	1.4	.971

TEN

Left-Handed Pitcher

IMAGINE IF THERE HAD NEVER BEEN a man named Harry Frazee, or if he had never owned the Boston Red Sox. Or imagine if this Harry Frazee had been more interested in baseball than he was in show business, or if his Broadway show, *No, No, Nanette*, had been an instant box-office success and he didn't need money to keep it going.

I don't think there's a Red Sox fan alive that hasn't imagined these things and, by doing so, rewritten baseball history.

Frazee was the guy who will live in Red Sox infamy because in 1920 he sold Babe Ruth to the Yankees so he could bankroll his Broadway show, which was his first love.

At the time, the Red Sox had won six pennants and five World Series (there was no World Series in 1904), more than any other team. And the Yankees had won none. What would

1. BABE RUTH

2. LEFTY GROVE

3. MEL PARNELL

4. BRUCE HURST

5. BILL LEE

have happened if Frazee hadn't needed the money he got from the Yankees in the sale of Babe Ruth? Would the Red Sox now be the team that has won 39 pennants and 26 World Series instead of the Yankees? Sox fans like to think they would be.

124

Few people realize that before he became the game's greatest slugger, Babe Ruth was considered the best left-handed pitcher in the American League.

Those who take the other side of the argument point out that with the Red Sox, Ruth was a pitcher, and had he stayed in Boston he might never have become the greatest slugger in baseball history. Hold on there just a minute. While he was in Boston, and possibly the Red Sox's best pitcher, Babe was already beginning to make his mark as a hitter. In 1915, when he was still strictly a pitcher, Ruth hit four home runs. The league leader hit seven. By 1918, the Red Sox began to recognize what an offensive weapon they had in Ruth. Babe won 13 games as a pitcher, and he also played 59 games in the outfield and 13 at first base, and he tied for the league lead in home runs with 11. The following year, his last in Boston, he won nine games as a pitcher, but the Red Sox were beginning to use him more as an everyday player. He played 111 games in the outfield and 4 at first base and led the league with 29 home runs.

The game was changing, and Babe was the reason for the change. The manager of the Red Sox in those days was Ed Barrow, and it was Barrow who recognized the game was changing and who also saw what an offensive weapon he had in Ruth. Barrow is the one who began to use Babe more and more in the outfield. A year after Ruth was sold, Barrow became the general manager of the Yankees, and with Barrow calling the shots (making trades and building a farm system) and Babe hitting the shots (54 home runs in 1920, 59 in 1921, 60 in 1927), the Yankees won six pennants and three World Series over the next eight years. Red Sox fans like to think that if Ruth had stayed in Boston, a shrewd baseball man like Ed Barrow would have moved him to the outfield permanently and that success might have happened to their team. Who's to say it wouldn't have?

You talk about baseball and Babe Ruth is number one. *Numero uno!* To me, Ruth has to be number one among all-time Red Sox left-handed pitchers even though his career in Boston and his career as a pitcher were so short. He came to the Red Sox from Baltimore in 1914 and was 2–1 in his rookie year. The next year he won 18 games. In 1916, he was 23–12, third in the league in wins behind Walter Johnson (25) and Bob Shawkey (24). He then pitched 14 innings and beat the Dodgers, 2–1, in the second game of the World Series, which started him on a streak of 290 consecutive scoreless innings that stood as the World Series record until Whitey Ford broke it in 1961.

In 1917, his last year as a full-time pitcher, Babe was 24–13, second in the league in wins to Ed Cicotte's 28. Ruth was generally regarded as the best left-handed pitcher in the American League. His career record as a pitcher after the 1917 season was 67–34. He was only 22 years old at the time.

I had the good fortune of actually meeting Babe Ruth once. It was in 1943 and I was in the navy, playing with a team of major league all-stars, players like Ted Williams, Johnny Sain, Buddy Hassett, and Harry Craft. We had come up from Chapel Hill to play in Yankee Stadium in an exhibition game against a team of Yankees and Indians to raise money for war bonds. The Babe was there. I had never seen him before. I was impressed by his size, about 6′3″. I never realized he was so big. It was a hot day and he had on this beautiful white linen suit. He was dressed beautifully.

I think he was sick at the time because he was bent over, but he still was a big, powerful man. He died five years later. He came into our dugout because he knew some of the guys on our ballclub, and he shook hands with all of us. When he got to me he said in that gravelly voice of his, "Hiya kid, how are you?"

He didn't know anything about me, but I certainly knew him.

By the time **Lefty Grove** arrived in Boston in 1934, he had already had a Hall of Fame career. He also had a sore arm. In Philadelphia, Grove led the league in wins four times, in earned run average five times, and in strikeouts seven years in a row. He was a hard thrower, but when he got to the Red Sox and hurt his arm, he had to learn to be a pitcher.

He learned so well that he won 20 games in 1935, led the league in ERA four more times, and had a record of 105–62 in his eight seasons in Boston. In the final appearance of his career, in a Red Sox uniform, Grove won his 300th game. That was in 1941, the year before I got to Boston, so while I did get to meet the great Lefty Grove, I regret that I just missed the opportunity to be a teammate of one of the legendary pitchers in baseball history.

He [Lefty Grove] was a hard thrower, but when he got to the Red Sox and hurt his arm, he had to learn to be a pitcher. He learned so well that he won 20 games in 1935, led the league in ERA four more times, and had a record of 105–62 in his eight seasons in Boston.

126

In my 60 years with the Red Sox, I never saw a left-handed pitcher handle Fenway Park as successfully as did **Mel Parnell**, the gentleman southpaw from New Orleans. Fenway, with its frightening left-field wall, the "Green Monster," hovering only a pop fly away from home plate, was death to lefties. But not to Parnell, who had a career record of 70–30 there and just 53–45 in all the other American League parks.

That's Lefty Grove of the Red Sox shaking hands with Dizzy Dean of the Cardinals—the
starting pitchers in the 1936 All-Star Game in Fenway Park. Even though he came to
Boston late in his career, Lefty Grove still won 105 games, including number 300, in a Red
Sox uniform.

(From left) Ted, Mel Parnell, and me after Mel beat the Yankees for his 25th win in 1949. If he'd had just one more win in him on his next start, we would have gone to the World Series that year.

Mel came to us in 1947. The next year he was 15–8. Jack Kramer won 18 games and Joe Dobson won 16, but Mel was our best pitcher in the second half, and when we finished the regular season tied with Cleveland, which meant a one-game playoff, most of us assumed Parnell would get the ball from manager Joe McCarthy in the playoff game. Parnell was in his first full season and had not yet established himself as a left-hander who could win in Fenway Park, where the playoff game was to be played. So McCarthy went for a veteran and well-rested right-hander, Denny Galehouse, who was 8–8, to start for us.

The Indians defied tradition, logic, and the Green Monster by starting Gene Bearden, not only a left-hander but also a rookie. They beat us, 8–3, and they went to the World Series instead of us. To this day, most of us believe things would have been different if McCarthy had chosen Parnell to start that playoff game.

In 1949, Parnell led the American League with 25 wins, a 2.77 earned run average, 27 complete games, and 295N innings. That was the year we fell behind the Yankees by five games with three weeks left in the season. With our pitching staff riddled with injuries, Joe McCarthy put the pitching load on his two most reliable and able-bodied pitchers, Parnell and Ellis Kinder. Between them, they started 10 of our last 19 games and relieved in 7 others.

We went to Yankee Stadium for the final two games of the season, leading the Yankees by one game in the standings. All we had to do was win one of the two and we would win the American League pennant. And we had our two best pitchers, Parnell and Kinder, set up to pitch those final two games. We were certain we would win at least one of the two games.

Parnell wasn't a big guy to begin with, 6', about 185 pounds. Pitching almost every day, his weight had dropped to 160 by the time he faced the Yankees in the next-to-last game of the season on Saturday, October 2. We jumped out in front and led 4–0, but Parnell was just worn out and couldn't hold the lead. We lost that game, and the Sunday game, and another pennant slipped from our grasp.

After 1949, Parnell was never the same pitcher, although he did win 69 games over the next four seasons, including 21 in 1953. From then on, he pitched with a bad elbow and won only 12 games in his last three years. But one of his wins in his final season, 1956, was the Red Sox's first no-hitter in 33 years. When he retired, Parnell had a record of 123–75 and a winning percentage of .621 for his 10-year major league career, all with the Red Sox.

On a personal note, I'm indebted to Mel for helping to keep my name alive. After he retired, Parnell joined Ken Coleman and Ned Martin on the Red Sox radio team. One day, somebody hit a ball off the right-field foul pole and Mel said, "That's Pesky's pole."

I wasn't a home-run hitter—I hit just 17 in my career—and when I hit one, it usually was down the line in right field, the shortest part of the ballpark. Mel explained that I hit a few in Fenway Park that just scraped the right-field foul pole and so the players began to call the right-field foul pole "Pesky's Pole." The next thing you know, it caught on and people began calling the right-field foul pole in Fenway Park "the Pesky Pole." I still hear it to this day. Recently, I heard Joe Buck on Fox mention the "Pesky Pole."

*D*ominic DiMaggio remembered Mel Parnell, the classy lefty, as a pitcher of guile and courage, a big winner for the Red Sox in Fenway Park, where left-handers rarely succeeded. He remembered, too, when he first noticed the change that turned Parnell into a big winner. It was in the spring of 1948, and DiMaggio remembered it because that was the year Joe McCarthy, who had managed the Yankees to so many triumphs, took over as manager of the Red Sox.

Parnell was a young left-hander out of New Orleans who had not yet lived up to his great promise. He had come to Boston the previous season, a rookie who appeared in 15 games, most of them in relief, had a record of 2–3, and had a hideous earned run average of 6.39—in other words, nothing that would inspire great expectations.

"One day he was pitching batting practice," DiMaggio remembered, "and I stepped into the cage to take my swings. He looked different. Everything he threw came in on my hands. I was breaking bats and hitting everything off the fists. I was afraid of getting a bone bruise. I said to him, 'Mel, you're throwing sliders.'

"'No I'm not, Dom,' he said. 'I'm just throwing naturally.'

"I think he had something wrong with one of his fingers. It was crooked or something. Whatever it was, it gave his ball a natural movement that came in on a right-handed hitter. He also could make the ball tail away from a right-handed hitter, and that's what made him so successful, especially in Fenway Park."

Parnell went on to win 15 games that season, played 16 complete games, and cut his ERA in half to 3.14. By the second half of the season, he was the Red Sox's most dependable pitcher, which is why it was so surprising that McCarthy chose veteran right-hander Denny Galehouse, and not Parnell, to pitch the one-game playoff against Cleveland in Fenway Park for the American League pennant.

"We all wondered why McCarthy picked Galehouse to pitch that game instead of Mel, or Ellis Kinder," DiMaggio said more than a half century later.

"No reason was ever given. Maybe it was just a case of McCarthy waiting for somebody to ask for the ball and nobody did, so he went with the veteran."

Parnell went on to lead the American League in 1949 with 25 wins, 27 complete games, and 295.1 innings. He would win 21 games in 1953 and finish his Red Sox career with a record of 123–75.

"I liked playing behind him," DiMaggio said. "He made it fairly easy to play center field when he was pitching. Especially in Fenway Park."

That's flattering to me, and I have my old teammate, Mel Parnell, to thank for starting it.

What Mel Parnell was in the forties and fifties, **Bruce Hurst** was in the eighties, a left-handed pitcher who was more successful in Fenway Park than he was in other ballparks. Hurst got 56 of his 88 Red Sox wins in Fenway. Among Sox left-handers, only Parnell won more games at home.

In the 1986 World Series against the Mets, Bruce won Game 1 with eight shutout innings, then came back to pitch a complete game and beat the Mets and Doc Gooden, 4–2, in Game 5. In Game 6, the Red Sox took a one-run lead into the bottom of the tenth. When the first two Mets went out, the Shea Stadium message board flashed the words "Congratulations Red Sox." In the press box, word was being circulated that Hurst had been named the Most Valuable Player of the Series. Then came three straight hits by the Mets, a wild pitch, and a ground ball to Bill Buckner . . . but let's not bring that up again.

Once you get past Babe Ruth, Lefty Grove, Mel Parnell, and Bruce Hurst, the pickings are slim for left-handed pitchers with the Red Sox. There were Herb Pennock, Mickey Harris, John Tudor, and Bill Lee.

Pennock was a fine gentleman whom I got to meet later in his life. He became a Hall of Famer, but that was after he was sold to the Yankees (another one) in 1923. He had only 59 of his 240 major league wins with the Red Sox.

Harris had only one big year in Boston, 1946, when he won 17 games. We would not have won the pennant without him. But he won only 26 more games in parts of six seasons in Boston.

Tudor had a couple of good seasons in Boston, but he became an outstanding pitcher after he left the Red Sox and won 21 games for the Cardinals in 1985.

Bill Lee was as flaky as they come, your typical left-hander, but he was an outstanding pitcher who won 94 games with the Red Sox including three consecutive seasons with 17 wins, so he's number five on my list of the top five Red Sox left-handed pitchers.

Like Parnell, Bruce Hurst defied logic as a left-hander who truly excelled more in Fenway Park than he did elsewhere.

Bill Lee's flaky behavior often overshadowed his excellent pitching, which was good enough for 94 wins in a Sox uniform.

Statistical Summaries

All statistics are for player's Red Sox career only.

PITCHING

G = Games
W = Games won
L = Games lost
PCT = Winning percentage
SV = Saves
SO = Strikeouts
ERA = Earned run average

Left-Handed Pitcher	Years	G	W	L	PCT	SHO	SO	ERA
Babe Ruth *Led A.L. in games started, shutouts, and ERA in 1916*	1914–19	141	89	46	.659	17	453	2.19
Lefty Grove *Won team-record 20 straight decisions at Fenway Park from 1938–40*	1934–41	214	105	62	.629	15	743	3.34
Mel Parnell *Only Red Sox lefty to lead A.L. in wins (1949)*	1947–56	289	123	75	.621	20	732	3.50

(continued)	Years	G	W	L	PCT	SHO	SO	ERA
Bruce Hurst *Won over 10 games each of his last six seasons with Red Sox*	1980–88	237	88	73	.547	13	1,043	4.23
Bill Lee *Had seven wins and five saves as a reliever in 1972*	1969–78	321	94	68	.580	7	578	3.64

FIELDING

PO = Put-outs

A = Assists

E = Errors

DP = Double plays

TC/G = Total chances divided by games played

FA = Fielding average

Left-Handed Pitcher	PO	A	E	DP	TC/G	FA
Babe Ruth	92	347	15	19	3.2	.967
Lefty Grove	16	244	16	10	1.3	.942
Mel Parnell	69	327	12	27	1.4	.971
Bruce Hurst	66	207	11	8	1.2	.961
Bill Lee	53	325	27	19	1.3	.933

ELEVEN

Relief Pitcher

Ralph Houk called **Dick Radatz**, "the Monster," the best relief pitcher he ever saw, and I agree. For 1962–1965, he was as good as any relief pitcher I ever saw. Radatz was dominant, overpowering, and an intimidator. And that was in the days when relief pitchers—closers—pitched two or three innings and came in when the game was on the line, whether it was the ninth inning, the eighth inning, or the seventh inning. Sometimes, they were even used in the sixth inning.

It was not like today, when saves are cheap. Today, most closers never leave the bullpen until the ninth inning, and often they're being brought in to start the inning, not when there are men on base, not when there's trouble. To me, that cheapens saves.

1. Dick Radatz

2. Bob Stanley

3. Ellis Kinder

4. Sparky Lyle

5. Tom Gordon

Guys like Radatz, Joe Page, Sparky Lyle, Goose Gossage, and Rollie Fingers often would pitch two and three innings. That's why their saves totals were not as high as those of today's closers. But they won more games than today's closers.

If you want a more recent comparison for Radatz, he was like Gossage. Radatz was big, 6'6", 230 pounds, and he could throw hard. They didn't have

Dick Radatz was not only a monster of a man, but also the best reliever I ever saw.

radar guns in those days, but I'm sure he got it up to 98, 99 miles an hour. He may even have broken 100 at times. He'd stand on that mound, a towering figure, and he must have appeared as big as a mountain to hitters. And he was mean. He'd throw at you as soon as look at you. He terrified hitters. He'd just rear back and pump that fastball, and nobody ever hit him. They couldn't hit him. That's all he had, a fastball. But that was enough.

I first saw Radatz at the Red Sox minor league complex in Deland, Florida, in the spring of 1961. I was managing Seattle, the Sox's Triple A team in the Pacific Coast League, and Radatz was a starting pitcher at the time. He had been sent down to Double A ball the year before after starting out the season with Gene Mauch in Minneapolis, the Red Sox's other Triple A team in the American Association (in those days, it was not uncommon for teams to have two, and even three, Triple A clubs in their farm system), and he was going to be on my staff in Seattle. I had Radatz, Galen Cisco, Don Schwall, and Earl Wilson—a pretty good pitching staff for a Triple A team.

He [Dick Radatz] would stand on that mound, a towering figure, and he must have appeared as big as a mountain to hitters. And he was mean. He'd throw at you as soon as look at you. He terrified hitters. He'd just rear back and pump that fastball, and nobody ever hit him. They couldn't hit him. That's all he had, a fastball. But that was enough.

Harry Dorish was my pitching coach, and he said to me, "You know, Johnny, Radatz had some elbow problems last year."

I said, "Let's wait a few days and see if he's all right before we send him out there."

After about 10 or 12 days into spring training, Dorish said, "Johnny, we've got to find out if this guy can pitch."

I told Harry, "You stay with him, let him throw, and let me know when he's ready to pitch."

After a couple of days, Dorish said Radatz was ready, and I asked Harry, "What do you want to do with this guy? You're the pitching coach; you know more about it than I do." I suggested to Dorish we bring Radatz in during an inning and Harry said, "Let's start him."

So we started him against Toronto, which was managed by Charlie Dressen. Radatz pitched three innings and struck out all nine guys. When I saw this, I lit up like a Roman candle. We had another week or 10 days to set up our ballclub, but I let a day pass and then I called Radatz into my office.

"Did you ever think about relieving?"

"Oh, no, Johnny," he said. "I don't want to do that."

139

I said, "Oh, really? I'm surprised to hear that." And then I named three or four guys who were relief pitchers in the big leagues, and I said, "The game is changing, and these days relief pitchers are making as much money as a 15- or 18-game winner. You can be so good." Then I said, "Lookit, I'm going to take you with me no matter what. I don't care if you throw up on the pitcher's mound. But I'd like you to relieve."

He said, "But, Johnny, I don't know anything about relieving. I've never done it."

"I'll teach you," I said.

Imagine me teaching Dick Radatz to relieve! The way he threw the ball, it didn't take a genius to recognize how great he could be.

I said, "I'll make a deal with you. I'll try you in the bullpen, but if one of my top five starters doesn't pitch well, I'll give you a start."

"That's fair enough," he said.

We opened the season in San Diego. Don Schwall started, and it was one of those 4–3, 5–3 games. We were winning, and even though we didn't count pitches in those days, you just knew that Schwall had thrown a lot of pitches. I went out to the mound and asked Schwall, "How are you?"

"I'm OK, Johnny," he said.

I said, "I know you're OK, but how do you feel? The big guy's warming up, and I have to find out if he can do this or not."

So I brought in Radatz; he shut them out, and we won the game. Next we went to Salt Lake City. Bob Kennedy was the general manager and Freddie Fitzsimmons was the manager of Salt Lake. We were in the eighth inning, and I needed the big boy. He came in and bing . . . bing . . . bing . . . bing . . . game's over, we win.

The next night, we scored some runs, so I didn't need Radatz, and I didn't need him in the next series against Tacoma, a Giants farm team with Willie McCovey, Tom Haller, and Chuck Hiller. Then we went to Hawaii for a week. Seven games. First night, we won and Radatz saved the game. Second night, we scored enough runs, so I didn't need him. Third night, Schwall was on the mound and we were leading by two runs going to the bottom of the eighth, and I went to the mound to take out Schwall and bring in Radatz. In those days, the reliever came in from the bullpen in a golf cart. I was talking to Schwall, and I heard laughter coming from the stands. I asked Schwall what they were laughing at and Don said, "Radatz just fell out of the cart."

Radatz came to the mound and Schwall handed me the ball and I said to Radatz, "Do you think you can stand up long enough to get this next guy out?"

Radatz said, "Give me the ball and get your ass back in the dugout."

We won all seven games in Hawaii, and Radatz was in five of them. When they got the reports in Boston and they saw that Radatz was in almost every day, they said, "What's that Pesky doing out there?"

I said, "Well, you want me to win, don't you?"

And that was the start of Dick Radatz's career as a relief pitcher. The next year, he was in Boston and won nine games, all in relief, and led the league with 24 saves, when 24 saves were a lot. As an example, the number two man in saves in the American League that year, 1962, was Marshall Bridges of the Yankees with 18.

In his first four years with the Red Sox, Radatz won 49 games and saved 100 and never started a game. When he lost a couple of feet off his fastball, Radatz was no longer "the Monster," no longer the dominant relief pitcher of his time, and the Red Sox traded him to Cleveland. But for those four years in Boston, he was as good as I've ever seen coming out of the bullpen.

It's one of the sad ironies of baseball that **Bob Stanley**, who probably threw 4,000 pitches in a 12-year career, all with the Red Sox, should be remembered only for two of those 4,000 pitches. Both of them came in the tenth inning of Game 6 of the 1986 World Series against the Mets.

I'm sure you remember the game. The Red Sox were ahead in the Series, three games to two, and were going for the knockout punch in Shea Stadium. After nine innings, the score was 3–3, but in the top of the tenth, the Sox scored two runs, and when the first two Mets went down in the bottom of the tenth, the Red Sox were just one out away from ending a 68-year jinx by winning their first World Series since 1918.

Here's where bad breaks and fate intervened once again.

Three straight singles gave the Mets a run and made it 5–4 with the tying run on third and the winning run on first. In came Stanley, Boston's top reliever who had saved 16 games during the regular season, had saved Game 2 of the World Series, and had not allowed a run in three previous appearances in that Series.

Bob Stanley is the career saves leader for the Red Sox, but many fans only remember him for two pitches he threw in the disastrous 1986 World Series.

With Mookie Wilson at bat, Stanley threw a pitch that skipped past catcher Rich Gedman, allowing the tying run to score and the winning run to go to second. Officially, it was called a wild pitch, charged to Stanley, but most writers covering the game said they believed it should have been scored a passed ball. Stanley then got Wilson to hit an easy roller to first base that looked like, and should have been, the final out of the inning. But again the Red Sox jinx came into play. The ball trickled through Buckner's legs, and the Mets scored the winning run and then won Game 7, prolonging the Red Sox jinx and their World Series drought.

As a result, Bob Stanley, who would have been a big hero in Boston had he saved Game 6 and clinched the World Series, instead became another of the Red Sox players who would live in infamy all because of two pitches. It's unfair.

Bill Buckner was a lifetime .289 hitter who drove in more than 1,200 runs, but he's remembered for one ground ball.

Mike Torrez won 185 major league games and was a 20-game winner in 1975, but he's remembered for one pitch to Bucky Dent.

Ralph Branca won 21 games at the age of 21, but he's remembered for one pitch to Bobby Thomson.

And a certain shortstop I know led the American League in hits in each of his first three seasons, yet he's best remembered for holding onto the ball in the seventh game of the 1946 World Series.

Bob Stanley is number one on the Red Sox all-time list of saves (132) and wins in relief (85). He's pitched in more games (637) than any pitcher in Red Sox history, almost twice as many as the number two guy, Roger Clemens (383). He's in the Red Sox Hall of Fame, and he was a two-time All-Star. Yet, his legacy is two pitches in the tenth inning of the 1986 World Series, and to me that's unfair. You don't measure a man's career, his body of work, by just two pitches.

Ellis Kinder, "Old Folks," third on my list of all-time Red Sox relievers, was the kind of pitcher that's extinct in baseball today—a guy who started *and* relieved. The pitcher he most reminded me of in that dual capacity was the Yankees' Allie Reynolds, who also started and relieved.

In those days, it was not uncommon for a starting pitcher to go to the bullpen between starts, something of a lost art in baseball. No manager worth his computer would think of doing such a thing these days. If he did, he'd have his owner, and the pitcher's agent, on his back in a hurry.

For four years, 1962–1965, Frank Malzone played alongside Dick Radatz, some 90 feet away, Malzone at third base watching hitters quake at the monster of a man standing imperiously atop the pitcher's mound. Malzone watched in awe as Radatz reared back and fired his blazing fastball past hitters who seemed to know they had no chance against "the Monster."

"For four years," said Malzone, "Radatz was as good as there was in the game of baseball. When he came in, we knew the game was over. He's the best I've ever seen coming out of the bullpen. And a great man."

On the mound, Radatz was all business, according to Malzone. He was an intimidator second to none.

"In New York, they used to talk about Ryne Duren, because he wore those thick glasses and he would throw the first warm-up pitch to the backstop," said Malzone. "Duren threw hard, but he could be hit. I never was afraid of guys that threw hard because as hard as they threw, they still had to throw it over the plate, but I never hit against Radatz. I saw guys who were intimidated by him. It was amazing just watching him.

"How hard did he throw? Who knows? In those days, we didn't have radar guns; they used to measure the speed of a pitch against a motorcycle. I'm sure some of the hitters thought he was throwing 100 miles an hour, and maybe he was. All I know is the ball got up there in a hurry. In the years he pitched against Mickey Mantle, Mantle might have hit two balls off him. Dick threw nothing but fastballs to Mantle batting left-handed, and there were a lot of times Mickey would be walking back to the dugout.

"That's all Radatz had, a fastball. Actually, he had two fastballs, one that rose and another one that ran away from a right-handed hitter, what they call a 'cutter' today. I once asked Dick if he threw a curveball, and he said, 'Yeah, when I was in high school.'

"Radatz became a pitcher when he got to the big leagues and Sal Maglie [the former great New York Giants pitcher who was the Red Sox pitching coach in 1962] helped him by getting him to get more use out of the rubber by pushing off. His arm whipped around and his ball just popped.

"Dick would come in and I'd go to the mound and say, 'Let's get out of here quick,' and we would. With Radatz, I never had a manager tell me to go to the mound and slow him down. When he got out there, Dick was the boss. I might go to the mound and say, 'Do you mind if I just go in and have a drink?' Because nobody ever hit me a ground ball when he was pitching. And he did it with such ease. Look at his strikeout ratio [in his four full seasons with the Red Sox, Radatz struck out 608 batters in 537 innings, or 10.13 strikeouts per nine innings].

"And he didn't just pitch one inning like they do today. Today's so-called closers are a joke. Dick would pitch three, four innings. Once we played a game in Detroit. Dick came in around the sixth or seventh, and the game went extra innings and he wound up pitching eight innings. Johnny Pesky was the manager and, the next day, Radatz went to Johnny and said, 'If you need me for an inning today, I'm ready.'"

Ellis Kinder was a baseball rarity in his day: he started *and* relieved games for much of his career, which lasted until he reached the age of 43.

Kinder was almost 32 when he broke into the major leagues with the old St. Louis Browns in 1946, and he went on to pitch until he was 43, often with spectacular results. The Red Sox got him in a trade in 1948, and he became our most dependable pitcher for the next few years.

In 1949, he appeared in 43 games—30 starts and 13 in relief—and was 23–6. He was our starting pitcher in the final game of the season at Yankee Stadium, with the Yankees and Red Sox tied for first place. Whoever won that final game would win the American League pennant.

"Give me three runs and I'll win," Ellis promised.

He left after eight innings, trailing 1–0, and we wound up losing the game, and the pennant, 5–4.

Kinder was used almost exclusively in relief in the final seven years of his career and led the league in appearances twice, including 69 games in 1953, a major league record at the time. Twice, in 1951 and 1953, he led the league in both relief wins and saves, and despite being primarily a starting pitcher in his first three years in Boston, he is third in saves on the Red Sox all-time list, behind Bob Stanley and Dick Radatz.

146

When you talk about the Yankees flimflamming the Red Sox out of a player, Babe Ruth, of course, is at the top of the list. Not too far behind, however, and even more of a source of irritation to Red Sox fans—because it was relatively recent—is **Sparky Lyle**.

At least with Ruth, as I mentioned earlier, there was some justification for letting him go. That was a deal made because of financial constraints on Red Sox owner Harry Frazee. There was no such excuse in letting Lyle get away. And that deal came back to haunt the Sox for years.

It happened in 1972. At the time, Lyle had established himself as one of the top relievers in the game. Pitching exclusively in relief, he had won 22 games and saved 69 for the Sox. But relief pitchers were not considered as valuable then as they are now, and the Red Sox felt they needed a hitter, especially a right-handed hitter, to compete in Fenway Park. And the Yankees had a good one available in Danny Cater, who had batted .301 and .276 in his two seasons in New York. He had hit only 10 home runs in the two years, but the Red Sox reasoned that it was because he was hitting in Yankee Stadium, with its huge left-center and center field, "Death Valley." They figured things would be different in Fenway. They weren't, and the Red Sox regretted the trade for years.

Sparky Lyle established himself as one of the top relievers in the game while with the Red Sox, only to be snatched up by the Yankees in an ill-advised, one-sided trade. Sound familiar?

I give my old skipper Ralph Houk (I was a player/coach for Houk when he managed Kansas City in the American Association) credit for that trade. Ralph, who was with the Yankees, was ahead of his time in recognizing the value of a relief pitcher, and I later found out he had coveted Lyle for years and pushed hard for the trade.

Tom "Flash" Gordon became a closer during his time in Boston, and led the league in 1998 with 46 saves.

In his first season in New York, Sparky led the league in saves with 35. He also won nine games in relief. The Red Sox leader in saves that year was Bill Lee with five.

Lyle went on to save 141 games for the Yankees in seven seasons and win a Cy Young Award. Meanwhile, Cater batted only .237 in his first season in Boston, and his time there was injury-filled. In three years with the Red Sox, Cater played in only 211 games, hit only 14 homers, and drove in 83. So Fenway Park and the Green Monster were no help to him, and you can easily see why Red Sox fans feel they are snakebitten when it comes to trades with the Yankees.

Some of the game's most successful relievers have passed through Boston, including Lee Smith, Jeff Reardon, Bill Campbell, and Ugie Urbina. But for number five on my all-time list, I have to go with Tom "Flash" Gordon, who was only 5′9″, but had that man-sized curveball. The Red Sox got him in 1996; two years later, he led the league in saves with 46, which stands as the Red Sox record.

Statistical Summaries

All statistics are for player's Red Sox career only.

PITCHING

G = Games

W = Games won

L = Games lost

PCT = Winning percentage

SV = Saves

SO = Strikeouts

ERA = Earned run average

Relief Pitcher	Years	G	W	L	PCT	SHO	SO	ERA
Dick Radatz *Had team record 16 victories in relief in 1964*	1962–66	286	49	34	.590	100	627	2.65
Bob Stanley *Highest single-season winning percentage in Red Sox history (.882) in 1978*	1977–89	637	115	97	.542	132	693	3.64
Ellis Kinder *Won 10 of 11 decisions in relief in 1951*	1948–55	365	86	52	.623	91	403	3.28

(continued)	Years	G	W	L	PCT	SHO	SO	ERA
Sparky Lyle *Appeared in 899 games in his major league career, all in relief*	1967–71	260	22	17	.564	69	275	2.85
Tom Gordon *Had A.L. record 54 consecutive saves over two seasons in 1998–99*	1996–99	201	25	25	.500	68	432	4.45

FIELDING

PO = Put-outs

A = Assists

E = Errors

DP = Double plays

TC/G = Total chances divided by games played

FA = Fielding average

Relief Pitcher	PO	A	E	DP	TC/G	FA
Dick Radatz	20	42	7	1	0.2	.899
Bob Stanley	122	357	24	38	0.8	.952
Ellis Kinder	42	143	7	7	0.5	.964
Sparky Lyle	13	47	6	4	0.3	.909
Tom Gordon	39	52	5	4	0.5	.948

TWELVE

Manager

Joe McCarthy managed the Red Sox for only two-and-a-half seasons, but in the short time he was in Boston he impressed me so much that I have no hesitation in saying he was the best manager I ever played for. And the smartest. McCarthy was just brilliant. He never missed anything on the ballfield, and he had an attention to detail and a memory for events of the past that was unmatched by any other manager I've ever been around.

Joe DiMaggio once said, "Never a day went by that you didn't learn something from McCarthy." I second the motion.

When the Red Sox hired McCarthy to manage in 1948, it was hailed as a coup in Boston. They had finally turned the tables on the Yankees and hired somebody away from New York.

Many longtime baseball observers have called McCarthy the greatest manager in baseball history. In 16 seasons as manager of the Yankees, from 1931 to 1946, McCarthy had won eight pennants and seven World Series and was second four times. The only time he finished below third was his next-to-last season, 1945, during World War II.

1. Joe McCarthy

2. Joe Cronin

3. Dick Williams

4. Don Zimmer

5. Ed Barrow

Ed Barrow brought McCarthy from the Cubs to the Yankees, but Barrow was gone in 1946 and Larry MacPhail was running the club. McCarthy and MacPhail never hit it off, and 35 games into the season, with the Yankees in second place, McCarthy resigned.

He was a very mild-mannered man. He never raised his voice, but he could be firm and tough. McCarthy was a man of strong likes and dislikes, but he was fair. I learned one thing about him. As long as you busted your butt and played hard, you'd never have any problem with him.

When he left the Yankees, Joe went home to his farm in upstate New York, presumably retired for good. But after the 1947 season, Joe Cronin was promoted from field manager of the Red Sox to general manager, and he reached out to McCarthy and coaxed him out of retirement to manage the team.

In Boston, McCarthy came within two games of winning pennants in his first two seasons. In 1948, we lost to Cleveland in the one-game playoff and McCarthy was criticized for starting the veteran Denny Galehouse, who had a record of 8–8, in the playoff game instead of Mel Parnell, a 15-game winner who had been our most dependable pitcher down the stretch. Presumably, McCarthy chose Galehouse, a right-hander, over Parnell, a left-hander, because he didn't want to pitch a left-hander in Fenway Park. We were beaten by Gene Bearden, who was not only a left-hander but also a rookie.

The following year, we went to New York for the final two games of the season with a one-game lead, and the Yankees won both games.

Despite these two disappointments, I still have the highest regard for McCarthy's managerial skills. He was a great influence on me. I loved to listen to him talk baseball, and I'm sure a lot of whatever baseball knowledge I have acquired through the years I learned from him. He was a very mild-mannered man. He never raised his voice, but he could be firm and tough. McCarthy was a man of strong likes and dislikes, but he was fair. I learned one thing about him. As long as you busted your butt and played hard, you'd never have any problem with him.

The criticism he received for the 1948 playoff game and losing the final two games to the Yankees, of all people, must have demoralized McCarthy because in 1950, with the team in fourth place after 59 games, he retired for good and was replaced by Steve O'Neill.

Though not in Boston for very long, Joe McCarthy (left, with Casey Stengel) was simply the greatest manager I've ever been around.

Joe Cronin's distinguished managerial career was only a small part of his successful life in baseball. Here Cronin (right) visits with Washington manager Bucky Harris in April 1935.

Joe Cronin owns a special place in my baseball life. Not only was he my first manager, he gave me a chance to play in 1942 when he was beginning to scale down his playing career, and he picked me to be his successor as Red Sox shortstop.

As a manager, Cronin wasn't very verbal. He just let you play. He hardly said anything to me that first spring training with the Red Sox, and it wasn't until the day before the season opener that he told me I had made the team and I would be the starting shortstop.

Cronin had a distinguished career in baseball. He was a Hall of Fame player, a pennant-winning manager (1946), general manager of the Red Sox for 11 years, and the president of the American League from 1959 to 1973, the first former player to be elected a league president.

Dick Williams was a hard-driving leader who had a tendency to wear out his welcome wherever he went. He did it in Boston, he did it in Oakland, he did it in California, and he did it in Montreal, San Diego, and Seattle. But you can't argue with success. He won four pennants and two World Series, and he's the only manager ever to win pennants with three different teams, the Red Sox, A's, and Padres.

Williams feuded with players, general managers, and owners. His motto was, "My way or the highway." But he won.

Dick had never managed in the big leagues when he became manager of the Red Sox in 1967. He took a team that was ninth in the American League the previous year and finished a game ahead of Detroit and Minnesota, and three games ahead of Chicago, in the closest pennant race in American League history, and then took the heavily favored Cardinals to seven games in the World Series.

Williams often clashed with his players, especially Carl Yastrzemski, but Yaz had his greatest season under Williams in 1967, when he won the Triple Crown in batting average, home runs, and runs batted in.

Eventually, it was his inability to get along with his players that cost Williams his job in Boston, and when the Red Sox failed to duplicate their 1967 success by finishing fourth and third the following two seasons, Williams was fired and replaced by Eddie Kasko.

Williams didn't manage for a year, and then he had his greatest success in Oakland, where he won three consecutive division titles, two pennants, and two World Series and then resigned.

ick Williams arrived in Oakland in 1971 to take over a young and improving team, but one desperately in need of leadership. They had finished second in the American League West to the Minnesota Twins in each of the previous two years, and what they needed most was a firm hand, a manager who could teach them how to win. Williams was just the man for the job.

He had spent three seasons as manager of the Red Sox, with whom he won a pennant in 1967, ending a 21-year drought in Boston. So he came to Oakland with a pedigree that caught the attention and earned the respect of the talented young Athletics: Catfish Hunter, Vida Blue, Rollie Fingers, Bert Campaneris, Sal Bando, Joe Rudi, Rick Monday, and the irrepressible Reggie Jackson.

"Dick Williams was the guy the Oakland A's of '71 really needed to help us understand winning, to pull the talent together with a bunch of young guys full of testosterone and vinegar, and to get us on the right road," Jackson said. "He was very much like a sergeant or a lieutenant, an enforcer to make us understand the sacrifice and discipline we needed to be a winning team. He absolutely stressed fundamentals, hitting the cutoff man, hitting behind the runner. Playing winning baseball. Playing as a professional. Playing baseball and thinking as a manager would.

"That's who Dick Williams was for me. He made an impact on our team with his personality and his toughness and his attention to detail. He came along at a time in my career where I was a wild, big talent that struck out a lot, and he taught me about sacrifice and discipline and winning; in other words, how to go about being a winner.

"He wasn't easy on players. He demanded excellence. But he wasn't hard to play for. He was easy to play for if you played hard and you played well. If you made a mistake, he'd get on your fanny for it. If you made a mistake playing hard, he got on you to correct the mistake. But if you made a mistake and you weren't playing hard, he was just livid. We had a bunch of guys who were a little wild. We were even called 'the Wild Bunch' at one time, so we needed a manager like a Dick Williams to instill that discipline. Gene

Mauch also would have been a good manager for that team. We needed a hard-nosed, fundamentally sound manager that could enforce rules and guidelines for players."

Under Williams, the A's won three straight division titles and two World Series; then he walked away from Oakland. But he had carved his niche.

"Dick deserves a lot of credit for our success," said Jackson. "Was he the only manager who could have won with us? Probably not. But he was the right guy for us at the right time. You don't know how to win unless somebody teaches you how to win, and Dick Williams taught us how to win."

Who lets a manager that has won three division titles, two pennants, and two World Series in three years get away? A's owner Charlie Finley, of course.

Don Zimmer rarely gets the credit he deserves as a manager with creativity and imagination. He was an innovator, a student of the game, and an excellent day-to-day manager.

Zim is a baseball lifer like me. He goes back in the game almost as long as I do and is still going strong, in uniform for more than 50 years. He's a baseball treasure.

In his four full seasons as manager of the Red Sox, Zimmer finished second twice, third once, and fourth once. He never won a pennant, and his enduring legacy as manager of the Sox, unfortunately and unfairly, is that he was in the dugout in 1978 when Bucky Dent hit the home run.

The year before, Zimmer had brought the Sox home three games behind the Yankees. People will remember that Zim's '78 team blew a 14½-game lead in July. What they fail to remember, however, is that the Red Sox were down by three games in the final week of the season and, to Zimmer's credit, came back to force a one-game playoff with the Yankees.

I can't tell you much about **Ed Barrow** as a manager. He managed the Red Sox for three seasons, the last being 1920. I was a year old at the time.

I know Barrow only from the pictures I've seen of him—a man with bushy eyebrows—and from what I've read about him as the architect of the great Yankees teams that won 14 pennants and 10 World Series from 1921 to 1945.

Dick Williams (right), shown here with St. Louis' Roger Maris before Game 2 of the 1967 World Series, tended to wear out his welcome despite the fact that he won everywhere he managed.

Barrow never played the game professionally. He started out as a news-paperman and then formed a partnership with Harry Stevens, the famous baseball concessionaire. He was an owner of minor league teams and a president of minor leagues. In 1903, Detroit made him manager, but he wasn't very successful, and he resigned after a dispute with his general manager.

He was out of baseball until 1910, when he became president of the Eastern League. The Red Sox made him their manager in 1918, and it was Barrow who recognized the hitting ability of a young left-handed pitcher named Babe Ruth. Barrow began to use the young lefty more and more in the outfield.

The Red Sox sold Ruth to the Yankees in 1920, Barrow's last year as manager of the Sox. The next year, he became general manager of the Yankees. Sounds a little fishy to me.

Barrow managed the Tigers for two seasons and the Red Sox for three, and the only time he finished higher than fifth was in 1918, when Boston won the American League pennant by two-and-a-half games over Cleveland and then defeated the Cubs in the World Series, four games to two. That's the last time the Red Sox won a World Series, and that, alone, is enough for me to make Ed Barrow number five on my all-time list of Red Sox managers.

I have had the privilege of playing for, or working with, every Red Sox manager from Joe Cronin to Grady Little (I even had the job myself in 1963 and '64, and again in 1980), and I have enjoyed my association with all of them.

I don't want to slight anybody, but it's only natural that I have had my favorites, like Eddie Kasko, Kevin Kennedy, and Ralph Houk. Kennedy won a division title in his first year but managed only one more season. I wish he had been around a little longer. I would have liked to see him manage the Red Sox for more than two years. I believe he would have done good things. Kevin is a very capable guy, and he's still young enough to get another shot somewhere. I'd like to see him get a good ballclub and show what he can do as a manager.

Houk was special to me. I loved him. I was a player/coach for him at Denver in the American Association, and he was a joy to be around, he was such a good baseball man. We had a good team in Denver, players like Marv Throneberry, Tony Kubek, Whitey Herzog, Woodie Held, Lou Skizas, Jim Fridley, Darrell Johnson, and Bobby Richardson, who was one of the best

Don Zimmer was the losing manager on this unforgettable day in 1978 when Bucky Dent's home run ended Boston's season in miserable fashion. He then figured prominently in another infamous clash with the Yankees 25 seasons later as a member of New York's coaching staff when he charged at Pedro Martinez in the 2003 ALCS. *Photo courtesy of Bettmann/Corbis.*

young infielders I ever saw. I played in about 90 games, pinch-hitting and playing part time. I was 36 at the time, and I hit .340. It was Houk who convinced me to manage. I didn't want to manage, but Houk convinced me to give it a try, and I did.

Houk was an outstanding manager for the Yankees, but unfortunately he never had that same success in Boston.

I have to mention John McNamara, who won a pennant in 1986, and Darrell Johnson, who won a pennant in 1975, and three guys I know nothing about. I didn't see them, of course, so I can't tell you much about Jimmy Collins, Jake Stahl, and Bill Carrigan.

Collins won back-to-back pennants in 1903–04, and the World Series in 1903. There was no World Series in 1904 because John McGraw, whose Giants won the National League pennant, refused to play the champions of the upstart American League, which was only three years old.

Stahl won a pennant and World Series in 1912. Carrigan won back-to-back pennants and World Series in 1915–16.

The Red Sox have won only 10 pennants, so I would be remiss if I didn't at least mention the managers of all 10 pennant winners—Collins, Stahl, Carrigan, Barrow, Cronin, Williams, Johnson, and McNamara—even if I don't place them among my top five Red Sox managers.

I would gladly revise my list to place as number one whichever manager leads the Red Sox to their next world championship. I just hope it's soon. And I hope I'm around to see it.

Ed Barrow (right, with Joe McCarthy in 1938) is generally credited with moving a young left-handed pitcher named Babe Ruth to the outfield to take full advantage of his hitting ability.

Statistical Summaries

All statistics are for manager's Red Sox career only.

MANAGING

G = Games managed

W = Games won

L = Games lost

PCT = Winning percentage

P = Pennants

WS = World Series victories

Managers	Years	G	W	L	PCT	P	WS
Joe McCarthy *Career .614 winning percentage is highest in major league history*	1948–50	369	223	145	.611	0	0
Joe Cronin *His 13 seasons is the longest tenure of any Red Sox manager*	1935–47	2,007	1,071	916	.539	1	0
Dick Williams *Finished first four times in his first six seasons as a major league manager*	1967–69	477	260	217	.545	1	0

(continued)	Years	G	W	L	PCT	P	WS
Don Zimmer *Won over 90 games each of his first three full seasons with Red Sox (1977–79)*	1976–80	715	411	304	.575	0	0
Ed Barrow *Only winning season in managerial career came in championship year of 1918*	1918–20	418	213	203	.512	1	1

Index